# BROKEN
## BUT NOT
## ABANDONED

MULTIPLE WOUNDS HEALED
BY THE MASTER'S HAND

## GLORIA MANNS

E xulon
ELITE

# TABLE OF CONTENTS

D edicated with love to my parents, my siblings, my loving husband, my four amazing children, my nine beautiful grandchildren, and my adorable great granddaughter, plus the two expected this year.

# INTRODUCTION

For several years I have been nudged by the Holy Spirit to write the story of my life. I have resisted with excuses such as: I'm not smart enough or who would want to read it, etc. Decision Magazine published my first article. The second was published by the Journal of Christian Nursing, but when the fourth one was rejected, I gave up. I didn't know then that authors have often had multiple rejections before having even one article accepted. I began to feel guilty for not obeying what I felt God was clearly instructing me to do.

One evening I had been asked to dinner by my friends Dr. Bruce and Beth Jones, a retired pastor and his wife. I accepted weeks before but was still surprised to find there were four or five other guests included in the dinner invitation. After dinner, Beth asked me if I was ready.

"Ready for what?" I asked.

"To give your testimony to our guests," she replied, puzzled by my confusion.

I had completely forgotten she had asked me to share when she invited me to dinner. One's testimony is what is in one's heart so I said, "Sure."

When I had finished telling my story, one lady told me I needed to write a book to encourage others who had experienced similar situations. I started to discount her suggestion when some of the others began agreeing with her. Pastor Bruce began to suggest titles and I was convicted that my disobedience was not honoring to God. Every devotional I read, every scripture I studied, and encouragement to write by several people convinced me that I needed to stop avoiding my assignment and begin.

My decision to proceed began in earnest on January 1st, 2014. Many doors opened for me that I couldn't have imagined ever would. You are now holding the finished product. Peace reigns in my heart as I know I have obeyed. It has been an exciting journey and I am so grateful for all of those who encouraged me along the way.

## THE TAPESTRY OF MY LIFE

My life is but a weaving
Between my Lord and Me.
I cannot choose the colors,
He worketh steadily.

Oft times He weaveth in sorrow,
And I, in foolish pride,
Forget He sees the upper
And I the underside.

Not til the loom is silent
And the shuttles cease to fly,
Shall God unroll the canvas
And explain the reason why.

The dark threads are as needful
In the Weaver's skillful hand,
As the threads of gold and silver
In the pattern He has planned.

He knows, He loves, He cares,
Nothing this truth can dim.
He gives the very best to those
Who leave the choice to Him.

—Author Unknown

# CHAPTER 1

When asked to tell the story of my life, it often seems like I'm talking about someone else. My question is; "Can God grab onto a messy child with a less than desirable beginning and make something brand new?" To quote Sarah Palin, "You betcha." My life is a testimony to God's amazing grace. Others have endured worse, of that I'm sure, but my story is unique to me and is God's story of His desire to make all things new, including this very damaged person.

I didn't know my parents' stories until later in life. When they married, dad was thirty-six and mom twenty. Mom had all the hopes and dreams of any young bride, and dad was ready to settle down. He had been married before and had a daughter about ten years old. When he got out of prison, he went to see his wife and daughter, and his wife slammed the door in his face, and that was the last he ever saw of either one of them. Dad was born to a wealthy Virginia family and was the only son. When his mother died at thirty-nine from breast cancer, his father remarried a woman who had a son. The new wife's son very quickly became the favored boy, and my dad felt discounted. He left home at sixteen. His story between then and when he met my mom is sketchy at best.

I was born eleven months after my parents married, and though dad wanted a boy, he was thrilled with his baby girl. However, he was very controlling about my care. "She's too warm. Why is she dressed like that?" were said in an accusing way to my mother. (Grandma told me this years later.) That might have been the beginning of my mom's resentment of me. It probably seemed to her that dad favored me over her. I think he was inadvertently pampering me in a way he might have wanted to his first daughter.

My brother Donny was born fourteen months later. I don't remember much until I was about four or five, and some of those memories are sweet. We lived in the country with a little creek running behind our home. Mom would take Donny and me there to let us play and then bathe us in the late afternoon. We were dressed in clean clothes in anticipation of dad coming home from work. Mom also had on clean clothes; her hair was done, and she wore make-up. Dinner was on the table when my dad walked through the door, and for the most part we were quiet during the meal while they discussed their day. On Sunday afternoons, dad would take us all to an ice cream stand for a treat. Sometimes he even let us ride in the back of his pickup truck, which was a real thrill.

I remember the evening that things seemed to be coming apart at the seams. Mom was washing dishes while looking out the window at my dad in the back yard by himself. His back was to her, and she was crying. Trying to help by attempting to reach and dry the dishes, I asked mom if she was okay. She said she was, but it was then the tension began to build in our home. They either fought or didn't speak.

Mom was already pregnant with my sister Janet, and she was born a few months later, just before my fifth birthday. I started school just before my sixth birthday, skipping kinder-garten and going directly to first grade. There were no school lunches then, and the first day of school my mother sent my lunch with milk in a baby bottle. She thought it was hilarious when I protested loudly. The kids made fun of me, and I told my mother that I didn't want any milk in my lunch pail. My first report card was all A's with one B. My father's only question was, "Why wasn't that B an A?" setting the tone for my grades throughout my life.

When Janet was about two, my job was to watch her when she was outside in the yard. One evening my parents went for a walk, and when they came back, they found that Janet had fallen and scraped her knee. My father immediately began yelling at me, "Why weren't you watching her?" I began to cry and was then spanked and sent to bed.

Mom was sick a lot with bad headaches and would often have a neighbor take her to the doctor for a shot three or four times in a day. She also took many pain pills. My job was to watch the other two kids while she slept for hours during the day. By the time I was eight and a half, my brother Roger was born, and Candi joined our family just after my tenth birthday.

My mother's headaches and trips to the doctor continued until she was in bed most of the day. Dad left for work just after 5 AM and returned about 6 PM. He was always mad, and I thought it was because I wasn't doing a good enough job taking care of the other four. Sometimes I called neighbors to help because my mother had tried to get out of bed and fallen. The neighbors were unhappy, and again I thought it was because I'd bothered them. Most of the time, I was just plain scared and trying to do my best.

That winter when Candi was three months old and Roger eighteen months, I stayed home from school for months because I was needed to care for the kids. I managed to get the older ones off to the school bus and then spent the day caring for the two babies. Roger was deaf from measles and pneumonia, but no one knew that then. Mid-afternoon I realized there were no more diapers for the babies, and I began using hand towels for diapers. Laundry needed to be done, but I had been warned to never touch the wringer washer on the back porch or the mangle in the kitchen. Desperate, I broke the rules, dragged the washer into the kitchen, and washed the diapers. A ten year old does not know much about laundry except that clothes get hung on the line outside. The babies were in their cribs, and I took the wet diapers outside in the middle of a snowstorm and hung them on the line. A few hours later, thinking they must be dry, went out to find them frozen stiff. I waited a few more hours and tried again with the same results, so brought them into the house and proceeded to run them through the mangle over and over again until they were dry. Needless to say, I was in big trouble with my dad when he got home. He was so angry, and words can't describe the defeat I felt. At one point my whole family was in the hospital. I had been in with measles and pneumonia but was the first one discharged. I was supposed to stay with a neighbor but left in the late evening to go to my own home. I crawled into my parent's bed and cried myself to sleep: young, alone, and afraid.

# CHAPTER 2

The following spring, my father left us, supposedly to run antiques to South Carolina. The babies went to a children's home, and the rest of us went into foster care, none of us together. The home I went to consisted of two parents and one girl two years older than me and another two years younger. I didn't know what to do with myself. I missed the babies so much; I went to school every day and didn't have to do anything much except make my bed and take my turn drying the dishes. Nothing felt normal to me, but I adjusted and by summer was behaving like a semi-normal ten year old. When school was out, the family planned on taking a summer vacation. The only problem was that I was not invited to join them and had to go to another foster home. I hadn't seen my father, and my mother was a governess for a girl my age in the same city.

The second foster home was a nightmare even though it was the only so-called Christian home I'd ever been in. My sister Janet was with me, and the foster parents were in their sixties. The house seemed dark inside all the time. We were in church four times a week and not allowed to see movies, play cards, or wear make-up. I was eleven and Janet six, so it wasn't as if we'd wear make-up. My job was to do the dishes, clean the house on Saturdays, and do the laundry for the whole family.

The second or third time I was in the cellar doing the laundry I heard someone coming down the stairs. I just kept running the clothes through the wringer so I could get done. Within what seemed like seconds, someone was standing behind me groping my developing body. I froze, too scared to even move or scream. It was the foster father, and he said if I told anyone, he'd do the same thing to my sister, so to protect her, I didn't. This activity continued until we left to go to an orphanage. I'd hear him coming and immediately tenaciously grab onto the rim of the washer. Although I tried to pretend it hadn't happened, I felt dirty and ashamed that somehow I had invited this behavior. I had no idea then how much it would affect my intimacy with my husband or my ability to breast feed my children. To this day, I still cringe when I'm in the cellar and hear footsteps on the stairs.

That summer I started my period, and although I knew what to expect, I didn't have any of the necessary supplies. The foster mother gave me an old rag to use and offered no further help. My mother was living in the same town, and I rode my bike right in front of her car to get her attention to tell her I needed stuff. She was driving to the beach with her charge in the back-seat, in a convertible with the top down and seemed annoyed at the inconvenience. She did, however, buy what I needed and then went merrily on her way, oblivious to my needs.

I have no recollection of leaving the foster home and going to the orphanage, which looked huge and cold: three stories tall and all built of field stone. The rooms seemed large and unfriendly. The campus consisted of the orphanage, an old folk's home, and an infirmary—three separate buildings of various sizes looking like three fortresses backed up by woods. I felt little, lost, and very alone. One evening pig hocks were served for dinner complete with rind and hair. Looking at it made me gag. Refusing to eat it, I was made to sit at the table until I finished, which I did not. Finally at 10 PM I was sent to bed. Normal bedtime was 8:30.

A window seat on the staircase became my favorite place to be. I could look out the front windows of the fortress awaiting my parents return to take me home. My heart ached for home even though it wasn't ideal. Donny and Janet were in the orphanage too, as well as two other sibling groups of two, but my baby sister Candi and brother Roger were elsewhere, and I missed them immensely. Being the oldest girl granted me no special privileges. Bedtimes and mealtimes were the same for all seven of us.

It was there that I began building a high tower of thick walls around my heart. At some level, I determined I would never let anyone get close enough to hurt me again.

Starting seventh grade in a new school with the stigma of being one of the orphanage kids did nothing to help my fractured self-worth. Whenever the man who managed the farm associated with the orphanage delivered produce to the kitchen,

I hid. He was kind and never inappropriate, but I still didn't trust him or any other man for that matter. The housemother was a widow in her seventies, and the cook was in her sixties. Neither taught me about personal hygiene, so body odor hovered all around me, which only made me feel worse. I bathed, but after gym class it was bad. I avoided being around anyone and isolated myself even more.

We lived there until I was almost fourteen. About six months before we left, a seventeen-year-old farmhand befriended me for a long time before I'd give him the time of day. He asked me to the movies several times, but I gave a resounding no. Eventually I dared to go after getting permission, but it was strictly a hands-off deal. He did hold my hand, but that was it. I was untouchable, but it was nice that someone paid attention to me. Thankfully it was a short relationship. I was too frightened.

# CHAPTER 3

J ust before school let out for the summer, my mother and
father reconciled, and we all moved to Buffalo into a fairly
new government housing development. The public school we
attended was across the street. I only attended that school for
one month as I was to start high school in September. Dad had
opened a new and used bookstore, but there wasn't enough
money, so we ended up on public assistance. I started high
school that year and made a few friends from the neighborhood.

Ben and me

Nine months later my brother Ben arrived. He called me
"mommy" until he was five because he didn't know any better.

I loved him dearly and treated him as if he was mine. Mom was no longer taking drugs but had switched to beer, lots of beer. Ben was my responsibility as were the rest of the kids plus laundry and cleaning. Once again my mother had taken to her bed for days and eventually weeks at a time. There was a well-baby clinic in the projects, and I knew Ben needed shots and wasn't getting them. One afternoon I cleaned him up and put on his and my best clothes and walked to the clinic. Marge, a wonderful nurse and mentor, asked if I were his mother. "No, but my mom is sick, my dad at work, and I know he needs shots," I replied. She examined him while telling me what a good job I was doing caring for him. After getting my dad to sign the permission papers later that week, I began taking Ben once a month for his check-ups. Marge was always very encouraging and is the one of the reasons I became a nurse. She even managed to get me a scholarship to a nursing school close to home. I will never forget her and the way she encouraged and validated a damaged fourteen year old. God's hand was all over that relationship. But I'd only let her get so close to me. I trusted no one.

Although I missed a lot of school due to being needed at home, I managed to make the honor roll all but three times during high school. I loved learning and getting good grades. My dad always praised me for doing well in school, and my mother degraded me, saying, "You think you're so smart; you're just too big for your britches." I couldn't please them both but kept getting the good grades. I was very shy and withdrawn most of the time, afraid really. By my senior year I had

had no dates and wasn't going to the senior prom by the look of things. My sister, on the other hand, was outgoing and popular, which pleased my mother immensely. One day when I had my nose in a book, she told me all I needed was a "good screwing" and I'd straighten out. What? I was devastated.

I began searching for God and because Catholicism was most familiar to me, I wanted to go to the cathedral on Sundays. Mom occasionally attended a Unitarian Church but rarely went. Dad never went to church that I can remember. My job was to drive all us kids to that church. I didn't like it after a few weeks, so dropped the other kids off and went two blocks to mass at the cathedral. I felt safe there, but something was still missing.

In the spring of my senior year in high school, I saw a young man walking down the street in front of our unit. I'd never seen him before and thought he must be new to the neighborhood. He was whistling and seemed to be in his own little world. Dark haired and muscular, his dimples were what had me take a second look. This became a daily event, and I began watching for him. One day as I stood in the doorway watching him, I told my mother I was going to marry him. I didn't even know his name, and mom thought that was the funniest thing she'd ever heard. However, my mother couldn't stand the fact that I didn't have a date for the prom, so she connived with a neighbor to find out who this young man was and to make sure we met, which we did on May 6, 1958, one of the best days of my life. According to him, he had seen me and wanted to meet "the girl in the next unit with a pony tail wearing a sweatshirt and shorts." His name was Dan Manns, the oldest boy in a family of six siblings. He was twenty-one and had just finished four years with the Coast Guard during the Korean War and was now home living with his mother and siblings. He had been the main supporter of his family throughout his tour of duty and continued to support them. His dad had a mental illness and was institutionalized on and off for most of Dan's life. We did go to the prom and had fun even when I fell out of a canoe the next day at a class picnic.

I chose to become a nurse mainly because of Marge's influence and encouragement. I knew I wanted to have a family one day and determined then that none of my children would ever be in foster care or an orphanage because I'd always have a job. I started nursing school the next year and had to live in the dorms with one overnight out allowed per month.

Student nurse

I missed my little brother Ben so much and had no idea then that it would not be the end of my caring for him. Shortly after starting school, my mother began to call and beg me to come home to help. She'd had another baby by then. So every day after classes or my clinical were done, I'd take the bus home, do laundry, dishes, bathe the kids, and get them to bed. Dad came home from work at 9 PM after a twelve-hour day and was annoyed that he had to drive me back to the dorm, approximately eight miles. One evening as he drove me back, we passed a gas station that had a 1952 Dodge for sale in the parking lot. Dad stopped abruptly, paid the $40.00 for the car, and told me now I could transport myself back and forth. I felt like he was telling me he was done with me. When I returned to the dorm, I'd do homework and study for exams. Years later my classmates told me they thought I was just spending all of my time with Dan.

Dan and I dated for a little over three years and had planned an October 1961 wedding, one month after I graduated. My desire had been to consummate our marriage on our wedding night. However, that didn't happen quite like I expected. One evening just before I was going out on a date with Dan, my parents had a huge fight, and somehow I got blamed. I don't even remember what it was about, but I remember feeling very defeated when I left with Dan. We went to a drive-in movie and I just didn't care about anything, including the movie. Totally shut down emotionally, I didn't even resist Dan's advances, and we wound up having sex after which I had the same shamed feeling I did when I was being abused. Four weeks later I knew

I was pregnant and was overwrought. My mother couldn't have been more delighted.

"Well the fair-haired princess finally screwed up, didn't she?" were my mother's words to me. She couldn't wait to tell my dad and watch the disappointment in him. Unfortunately my dad had a heart attack before either of us could tell him, which turned out to be a blessing in disguise. As he rested in the hospital, no one wanted to upset him. Dad was recovering nicely, and before he was discharged, I wanted to tell him what I had done. My mother had gone away for the weekend to a bowling tournament, and I decided to confess while he was still hospitalized in case he had another heart attack or setback. Besides, I didn't want my mother anywhere around when I talked to dad. Anxiety pierced me to my soul as I approached dad. When I finished telling him, with tears in his eyes, he said, "I don't condone what you've done but neither do I condemn you." Grace upon grace— for the first time in my life. He asked me if I loved Dan and if I wanted to marry him. Of course, I did. We had been engaged since Christmas, so for me it was a given that we'd marry. Only sooner than planned. Unbeknownst to me, my dad gave the marriage two years as he didn't think Dan was good enough for me. Somehow I think dad was living his life vicariously through me as he didn't have an education and knew that I was bright enough to be the doctor he hoped I would—not my dream, but his.

Dan felt horrible about my being pregnant, and I was just plain mad and not very nice about it. I wanted the baby, but I didn't want my being pregnant to be the reason we got married, so I told Dan that if he ever brought it up that he *had* to marry me, we were done. He cried when he thought for an instant I wasn't going to marry him. We met with the priest separately as was the tradition then. He saw me after he saw Dan, and among other questions he asked me if there was any reason why we had to get married. I said "no." To which he replied, "Now Gloria, we both know you're pregnant." I was furious. "If Dan told you he *had* to marry me, the wedding is off," I screamed. "I can raise this baby by myself and don't need him or anyone else," I rose to leave his office, but he asked me to stay and reassured me that Dan had said no such thing. We set a date for mid-June. Dad was well enough to walk me down the aisle and did so proudly. Dan's family of six siblings all had varied reactions to our news. His mom was amazing. She loved me for who I was and didn't expect anything from me, which was new, and I drank in all the love she lavished on me. She truly was God's gift to me, and I felt valued. Her reaction to my being pregnant was "like father, like son." She had also been pregnant when she married. Dan's dad had paranoid schizophrenia and had been in and out of a mental institution most of the thirty years they'd been married. She was poor but never complained and had managed to raise seven children on public assistance.

We honeymooned in Niagara Falls for three days as Dan had to go back to work for American Airlines, and I had to return to nursing school. Thankfully it was within three months of graduation, and the students could live at home if they desired.

Dan and I lived with my parents briefly. We found an apartment rather quickly as my mom still expected me to take care of her home and the kids. Our first apartment was adorable, and we loved it.

Our son Danny was born in early December and we were a poor but happy little family. Thankfully Dan's sister had had twin boys six months before Danny was born and gave me their outgrown clothes or our son may have been dressed in swaddling clothes.

Danny on his christening day

Our landlord and his wife lived upstairs and were a delightful couple who loved Danny like he was their own. I tried to breast feed Danny but unconscious memories of my abuse prevented it from being a pleasant experience. I lasted five weeks and stopped when he hit a growth spurt and wanted to eat more often. Thinking my milk wasn't good enough dovetailing on the overarching theme of my life, I quit and put him on formula. Two months later I was pregnant again and not very happy about it. I actually refused to believe I was pregnant for about six months. We had to move to a larger apartment as one bedroom wasn't sufficient for two babies and two adults.

Our daughter Kelly was born in November, eleven months after Danny. I didn't even try to breast feed her as I was sure I'd fail again. I loved my babies more than life itself and lavished in the special times set aside each day to focus totally on each one.

Kelly at two weeks old

I sure had my hands full but went back to work part-time to help with expenses. In the early sixties men hadn't been socialized to help with "women's work," and it was unusual for a mother to work outside the home. That led to my being tired and cranky most of the time. It never occurred to me to ask Dan for help with housework or childcare.

Eventually I was working full time—actually 6 night shifts a week— on two to three hours of sleep a day. Dan worked afternoons, so one morning when I got home from work, he told me he wanted me to start taking a nap before he left for work at 2 PM, and that he'd take care of the babies. That blew my mind! Even two more hours of sleep a day helped me to be less irritable.

# CHAPTER 4

My maternal grandmother lived in Auburn, New York, and I really loved her. One weekend we decided to visit her and introduce her to our babies. Dan fell in love with Central New York and asked me what I thought about moving from Buffalo. Family pressures were taking a toll on us, and we needed to be alone where we could grow as a family. Besides he loved fishing and hunting and the area had many lakes and places to hunt.

"How can we do that?" I asked.

"I'll request a lateral transfer from the airport in Buffalo to the one in Syracuse," he replied.

It was like a dream come true. We figured it would take at least eighteen months for the transfer to go through, but two weeks later he was to start in Syracuse. We found a house to rent near where I had lived as a child, and Dan commuted forty-three miles each day to Syracuse, which was really rough through the winter. I worked full time in a nursing home. As soon as Dan got home from work, I was out the door to my job. That arrangement lasted about six months. I wasn't crazy about my job and longed to work in a hospital. The commute was taking its toll on Dan, and we were both always overtired. One day Dan told me he had met a guy at work who was a real estate agent and asked what I thought about buying a house and moving closer to the airport.

"How can we afford a house? We don't have any money for a down payment." I asked.

"Let's just talk to him, okay, and see what we find out."

We bought the third house we looked at, a quaint two-bedroom Cape Cod with an unfinished second story. We didn't have any money to put down so the builder held a second mortgage for us, and my dad lent us two hundred dollars to use as a commitment to the builder. The builder had told us that we had a lot of potential and he liked us, so he was willing to take a chance. This was more of God's grace although we didn't recognize it at the time.

A few weeks before we were to close on the house and move, Dan found a lump in his groin about the size of a walnut late on Friday afternoon. It didn't hurt him so we didn't think too much of it until Sunday morning when it was the size of a grapefruit. He drove himself the seventeen miles to the emergency room and left me with the two babies at home.

A few hours later he called to say he was going to surgery and needed a few things. I called a friend I'd known since childhood, and we all drove to the hospital. She then took the babies back to her house. Dan had cat scratch fever that had caused his lymph node to enlarge. The doctor was going to remove the node, make a vaccine from the stuff inside it, and give it back to him to prevent this from ever happening again.

We had a couple of kittens that would climb up Dan's legs. Apparently one of them had scratched him, and that caused all the problems. As a result of his surgery, he couldn't lift anything, so we had to hire movers, which we really couldn't afford. We closed one day, moved two days later, and I started working full time in a hospital two days after that. We had seven dollars to our name after we paid the movers.

Dan was able to return to work within a week. The minute he got home from work, I left. It was that way for many years, which took a toll on both of us, emotionally and physically, plus there was little, if any, "our time." He worked evenings, and I had the night shift. I had a miscarriage one night at work, took a break, sat with my feet up, and then went back to work. There was no taking care of me. I didn't know how.

We had talked about having another child but weren't seriously considering it at that time. I had a hard time getting pregnant after that. When we finally decided, we were in pretty good shape financially to have another child. After Kelly was born I had gone on the pill, which was fairly new then. It had one hundred times the amount of estrogen current birth control pills contain.

After eighteen months of trying, we were finally pregnant and more ready than we had ever been. Danny was five and Kelly four, and both would be starting kindergarten about the time the baby was due. That summer, Ben called to ask if he could spend the summer with us. We were thrilled to have him with us. He went back home for the school year but came the next summer and didn't leave for ten years. My boy was home at last. Dan and I knew nothing about raising a teenager but learned quickly. Ben rarely gave us any trouble and seemed genuinely happy to be with what he called his family.

Michael was born two weeks after school started, and we all were delighted with him. Six weeks later, I was back to work. By then Dan helped more with things around the house, all except laundry, which was fine. He could change diapers, make formula, cook meals, and even clean up like a pro. We still didn't have a whole lot of couple time but did have some amazing camping trips that the kids say are some of their fondest memories.

Our family is growing.

Patrick was born just before Mike's second birthday. He had bilaterally clubbed feet but was otherwise healthy. We figured our luck was running out on having healthy kids, so decided not to have any more. I bled for nine months after the birth and even a D&C didn't help, so at age twenty-nine I had a hysterectomy. My reproductive organs had suffered from the high doses of estrogen and were in pretty sad shape. It is one thing to decide not to have more children and quite another when the choice is gone. Anxiety prevailed as I was wheeled to the operating room, but I only felt relief when all was said and done.

# CHAPTER 5

D elighted with our four children but very cramped in our little home, we made the decision to finish the second story for more bedrooms and a bathroom. We also put in an in-ground pool as Dan had quit the airlines and was trying to find his niche. Therefore vacations went on hold for a few years, so a pool was the next best thing. The kids loved it as did their friends.

Dan eventually joined a police force, went to the academy, and was a very happy man. We, however, weren't doing so well in our relationship. I didn't feel loved and made some stupid choices that almost wrecked what little was left of our fractured marriage. When Dan discovered that I had been unfaithful to him, I thought it was over. But, by God's grace and Dan's sincere love for me, he told me that he felt he must not be meeting my needs or none of this would have happened. I fell in love with him all over again that day. It took a long time for our relationship to mend, but it was stronger than ever when the wounds had healed.

Whenever I got in a bad place emotionally, I'd sing "Turn Your Eyes upon Jesus." Sometimes I'd cry it, scream it, sing it, or seethe it but it always focused me on what was important. I knew in my heart that we both needed to change and that was the hardest part of the whole deal. We went back to church then. I began to notice how couples our age were close to one another and seemed to like one another. Marriage Encounter had been the answer for each couple.

I convinced Dan to go to an informational meeting, which he did very reluctantly as it was way out of his comfort zone, and he thought we were doing just fine. "It's to make a good marriage even better," I kept repeating. In the middle of the presentation Dan blurted out, "Okay, I'll go." You could have heard a pin drop, and the presentation was only about half over. The closer it got to our Marriage Encounter weekend, the more uptight Dan became. I think he drove "code red" all the way there with his other foot on the brake. As soon as we checked into the hotel, he turned on the TV. "Great," I thought. "This is supposed to a weekend of learning to communicate."

We went to the group dinner that night and some of the rules of the weekend were (1) no TV, (2) only talk to your spouse except at meals, and (3) feelings are neither right nor wrong, good or bad; they just are. Wow. Dan had always had a hard time if I cried, and I had a hard time with his angry outbursts. We had a lot to learn, and we did. We were given a question to write about in a journal and then two to three hours to discuss our feelings about the issue that particular question stirred up. The whole experience transformed our marriage, and we continued the question and dialogue exercise for a few years after that.

Let the healing begin.

Mom and dad came from Reno to visit the whole family for Christmas that year and stayed with my sister Jan and her husband Ken. Our family stayed overnight with them too. One evening all of Jan and Ken's five and Dan and my four children were sitting at my dad's feet listening to him tell stories. I entered the room and heard him telling the children that he hadn't been a very good dad and that he felt badly about how fast his kids had to grow up. He further explained that we had all had too much responsibility at very young ages and how he wished he could have done better.

I felt so sad for him. The next week or so, I wrote him a long letter acknowledging that my childhood hadn't been ideal but that I forgave him and was grateful for how my growing up years had in fact made me into the woman I now was. My mother told me years later that he kept the letter in his top dresser drawer and read it every night before he went to bed. Somehow I think he must have felt the love and forgiveness and held onto it tightly.

I love how God has our lives all planned out even when we are making a mess of it. With Dan's support, I went back to school to get my baccalaureate degree in nursing; one course at a time was all I could handle with a family and a full time job. At the same time I felt a need to revisit the orphanage. As a teenager, I had often fantasized about not getting off the school bus at the orphanage but going to a real home. And when that happened, I would thumb my nose at the building as I passed. I must have had the same need but found myself driving onto the property instead of past it. It was no longer an orphanage but a rock and fossil museum. I asked to tour the building, and the folks on duty that day were reluctant to let me go upstairs but eventually they allowed me to. I saw where the castor marks were from my bed and was amazed at how small the place seemed now. Pain, hurt, rejection, and sadness assaulted me as I walked through the whole building. I knew I had to face all those issues or I would never be healed.

Numb and confused when I left, I journaled all that was going on in my mind and emotions, and when I returned home, I cried for two weeks. My poor family had no idea what was going on. They rarely saw me cry. A few weeks later Dan and

I went back to that orphanage together so I could somehow explain what had happened to me. He agreed to help me tear down the high, very thick wall that was all around my heart. "I've always thought you would only let me get so close," he said as tears streamed down his face. It broke my heart to know that I hadn't let him or any of the children get close enough to hurt me. I didn't know then how much the whole shutting down emotionally as a teenager had affected all of my relationships but most importantly those with my husband and children. Opening up more to them felt very scary, and many times I still backed away from them. I guess I always expected someone was going to hurt me again, but my armor needed removing. Baby steps paid off as my feelings of vulnerability began to wane. At times they'd crop up intensely, but knowing I was loved made all the difference, and I calmed down much more readily. Dan was amazing in his consistency in helping me heal.

# CHAPTER 6

M y friend Mary was a co-worker who had lived across the street from the hospital when she had her first baby. She barely made it to the hospital and then hemorrhaged afterwards. Within a year she and her husband bought a farm several miles north of the city. Her second pregnancy resulted in a miscarriage after which she hemorrhaged again. She had quit work to stay home with her son and was again pregnant. She wanted me to be with her in the delivery room with this baby too. The plan was for her and Rick to pick me up on the way to the hospital. One evening I was visiting with a group of neighborhood women when my sixteen-year-old daughter called to tell me Mary was on her way. Anticipating she'd have a quick delivery, I had brought home two cord clamps and a bulb syringe to suction the baby's nose and throat should he or she decide to make a rapid entry into this world. While I waited, I called Dan who was on duty as a police officer to watch out for us and if we were speeding to please give us an escort to the hospital. An unfamiliar car pulled into the driveway and assuming it was Mary, I went out. Three people were in the front of a mid-sized car, one of which was Mary. Asking the woman with her to get into the back so I could get into the front, I got in. Mary immediately said, "The baby's coming."

"Calm down and breathe, Mary; you'll be okay. Dan is waiting for us in the village." A few minutes later I asked her who the people with us were and where was Rick. She introduced the couple and said Rick was way up north butchering a cow with her father but was on his way. February 20 is cold in central New York, and all the breathing and excitement had steamed up the windows so when we got to the village, I wiped my side window to let Dan know it was us. He took off down the parkway and we followed closely. At the end of the parkway he turned around and headed back to the village. What? Mary kept saying she had to push, so I got on the floor to take a look at what was going on. I had handed the lady in the back a small brown paper bag with the cord clamps and bulb syringe in it and told her that if the baby was born the first thing I'd need was the bulb syringe. Because childbirth is so unpredictable and the possibility that this could go on all night with me having to work the next day, I had packed clean underwear and stockings in that small bag as well. The driver also didn't know the way to the hospital, so I was instructing him too. We got on the interstate and I could see the baby's head crowning. Not wanting Mary to deliver until we got closer to the hospital, I encouraged her to breathe and try not to push. If she hemorrhaged again, I wanted her as close to help as possible. Jonathon Richard was not about to wait any longer and was born at 9:20 PM with the cord around his neck twice. When I asked for the bulb syringe, the lady in the back started throwing everything, including my underwear and stockings all over but did eventually hand me what I needed. The driver still needed directions as we were now off the interstate. Jonathon was fine. I wrapped him in my jacket to keep him warm. There was such a sense of peace in the car that Mary and I marveled later that surely we had felt the presence of God. She did not hemorrhage, and both were healthy. When Jonathon's first child was born, he sent his mother and me one and a half dozen roses each. Jonathon means "gift from God." A few months later, I began to sense something was missing in my life and could not figure out what. Dan and I were doing better, the kids were doing well, we had a nice home, new car and lacked nothing, yet something was missing.

Not long after that, a friend of mine from work gave me a book to read called *The Liberation of Planet Earth*, by Hal Lindsay. Having no solid religious foundation, I sought answers to some questions I had. This book started with a twenty-page testimony of the author's salvation and then explained God's plan when he created the earth; how man had destroyed it by sin; and how Jesus had redeemed His creation by His death and resurrection. At the end of the book there was an invitation to accept Christ's redeeming death on the cross on my behalf. I was reading in bed; Dan was working nights, so I was alone. I got out of bed and went into my sewing room, got on my knees, and said," Lord, if you are who you say you are, I invite you into my heart as my Lord and Savior. Please forgive all my sins."

No bells went off, no lightening flashed, but an incredible peace washed over me such as I had never experienced. It was January 1978 I was born again, and I haven't been the same since. Not knowing any other Christians and having no direction but having an inexplicable thirst for the Word of God, I read voraciously. Gradually over several months I found a Bible study to attend and wrote everything being taught in the margins of my Bible. I tried to share what had happened with Dan, but he didn't want to hear any of it. "I was born a Catholic, and I'll always be a Catholic, so don't be trying to change that."

One afternoon Dan was doing some work under the hood of our car and swearing up a storm. In a very pompous way I said, "If you'd just give it to Jesus ..." He lost his temper and everyone within a six block radius knew he didn't want to hear any more of my "blankety-blank Jesus stuff." I went into my sewing room where my Bible was and sat down defeated. Now I don't believe in randomly opening the Bible for a word from God, but I did. It opened to I Peter 3. I didn't even know there was a first Peter in the Bible. I read, "In the same way, you wives be submissive to your own husbands so that even if any of them are disobedient to the word, they may be won without a word by the behavior of their wives, as they observe your quiet and respectful behavior" (I Pet. 3:1) RSV.

"You're telling me to shut up, Lord, aren't you?"

In my spirit I heard, "That's right Gloria. You become the woman I called you to be, and I'll take care of Dan. I died for him the same as I did for you, and I love him just as much as I love you." For the next year and a half, God began to change me and my expectations and attitude towards Dan. I began loosening my reins of control over the entire family and asking Dan for opinions and help in decision making.

Sometimes he tested me by being obstinate, and I retreated to the bathroom where I did an SOS. The Bible says I am a vessel of the Holy Spirit and when a vessel at sea gets in trouble the captain sends out an SOS. So I figured I could do the same.

One evening Dan and I had an argument that we had had at least a dozen times without a resolution. As I stormed off to the kitchen, I heard the Lord speak to me. "Go into the living room, put your arms around Dan's neck and tell him you love him."

"Love him! I don't even like him right now."

"Do you trust Me, Gloria?" He asked.

"Yes, Lord, you know I do, but You have to change my heart before I obey. I will not be a hypocrite."

Over the next few minutes God did a wondrous work in my heart, and by the time I started towards the living room, I truly did love Dan. When I approached Dan, he jumped about a foot. He must have thought I had a machete in my hand. I did as the Lord instructed and went back to the kitchen weeping and rejoicing. I learned that day that the joy of obedience is directly proportional to the amount of faith it takes to obey. I did the supper dishes praising the Lord and expecting nothing from Dan.

Twenty minutes later, Dan came into the kitchen, put his arms around me from behind, and whispered that we'd never have that argument again and apologized. We hugged, and I knew a great chasm had been bridged. I wish I could say we lived happily ever after, but we still had a lot of growing to do and a number of bridges to repair. I, again, got to the place where I was not happy with Dan, when the Lord told me He wanted me to think of one good quality of Dan's. It took me two days to come up with "he is faithful."

From then on I added a new positive thought about him each day, and before long, there weren't too many negative ones for me to dwell on. I didn't like that I was the one who had to change for things to be better, but truth be told, I was the one who needed to adjust my thinking and feeling about the man God had ordained to be my husband "until death do us part." It was then that Dan began to bring me a fresh red rose "for no particular reason other than I love you." I also received anywhere from one to twelve on my birthday, Mother's Day, or whenever he felt like it, always accompanied by a beautiful card.

More content with each other

That spring Jan, Ken, Dan, and I went to Nevada to visit my parents. They had retired to Reno a couple of years earlier. We were not surprised to find my mother's drinking was as bad as ever. What stunned us was how badly dad was doing. Financially he was trying to make his Social Security go further by gambling, which wasn't profitable. He was using a credit card to buy groceries (not common then) and was very depressed.

After we'd been there a few days, we all asked dad if he'd like to move back to New York to be closer to family who might be able to help him. Seeming hopeful, he agreed to let Jan and me try to see what we could each do in our respective communities to find subsidized housing for them. Jan and Ken weren't very successful, but things seemed to fall into place for us, and we were able to get them back home with subsidized housing about a mile from our home. Dad was delighted. He thoroughly enjoyed being near his grandchildren and having some respite from my mother.

A few months later dad asked me what was different about me. I knew but was scared to death to tell the man who had raised me with "religion is a crutch needed by weak people" that I had accepted Christ into my heart and felt like the whole world had been lifted from my shoulders. So, instead, I said, "Dad, I'm happy with my home and my job. Dan is a great husband and father, the kids are doing well, and I'm in a nurse practitioner program that I'm very excited about,"

To which he replied, "No, there's something more. I have never seen you so content and joyful." I took a deep breath and told him I had accepted Christ's finished work on the cross for me; that the Holy Spirit now lived in me and I felt whole for the first time in my life. He didn't say anything at all, but I could tell he was thinking about what I had said. I gave him a Bible.

A couple of weeks later dad asked me to meet with him once a week for a Bible study. Not believing my ears, I agreed. I'd only been a Christian for about eight months, and it felt like the blind leading the blind, but I wasn't blind, and the Holy Spirit taught us both.

We met weekly for the rest of the summer and into the fall. One night dad called me and asked me to come to his house right away. Thinking he was sick, I hurried. Dad was sitting in his chair with his Bible on his lap and jamming his finger onto a page. The moment I walked in he blurted, "How can I go back into my mother's womb and be born again? She's been dead over forty years." He was reading about Nicodemus and Jesus in John, chapter 3. Breathing a sigh of relief, I said, "Read further, Dad. Jesus explains it in the next few verses." We talked about what being born of the Spirit means, and he settled down. Thankfully I knew those verses and some of what they meant. I explained to him that when we accept Christ, we are no longer dead spiritually because of Adam's sin. We are restored to the original condition of Adam and Eve before they sinned against God. I went home smiling. God was working on my dad.

# CHAPTER 7

I continued to grow in my relationship with Jesus but began to not feel very well. I was more tired than usual and blaming it on school, work, home, and family. My thought was, "*if I can just get to the end of the year, school will be over, and I can rest.*" By the end of September I could hardly put one foot in front of the other but pressed on anyway. I was, after all, wonder woman, right? My midterm exam for the nurse practitioner program was on a Thursday in a week when I diagnosed myself with a virus that would be over soon. Unable to study on Wednesday night due to fatigue, I got up at 4 AM to study. Not having the energy to sit, I lay on the floor and reviewed the material. I passed the exam with a great grade and struggled through the next day and a half of classes. By Saturday I had pain in my abdomen that would not quit but felt better when I was able to lie down, which I did before I left class to go home.

I had to get home because I had four bushels of tomatoes to can over the weekend. So I cut up tomatoes for about twenty minutes until the pain got intolerable; lay down for twenty minutes, and started the routine all over again. Dan was so angry at me for not seeking medical help that he had stopped talking to me, and I knew he was worried.

Sunday morning Dan took the children to church, and I promised him that if I couldn't get the tomatoes through the canner by the time he got home, I'd go to an emergency room. Even as I attempted to do the canning, I knew it was a futile effort. The whites of my eyes were yellow, and I knew something was more wrong than fatigue. I called a nurse practitioner colleague who was working that day and asked if she'd see me in a classroom before I went to the ER. She agreed. I was so afraid of there not being anything wrong and me just a big baby that I had to have her check.

She took one look at me and escorted me right to the ER. My liver was huge, and after two or three days in the hospital, a bone marrow biopsy, and blood transfusions, the diagnosis was chronic lymphocytic leukemia with an autoimmune antibody on my red cells, which caused the anemia and extreme fatigue. During my hospital stay, the director of nursing and the NP program visited me and promptly told me she would not allow me to finish the program. She was not compassionate and had no time for my pleading. I could almost feel some of my wall of protection going up again. The next four months were awful.

I felt like Wonder Woman had been struck off the wall and spent a lot of time with the Lord. By the end of that time, I knew my priorities were messed up. Work, school, and goals were what kept me going and the family got what was left over. I am so thankful for that time—even for the diagnosis—as all of it made me realize how superficial I had become, and it sad-dened me to my core.

My new priorities became: God, Dan, the children, extended family, work, school, friends, and goals. I did go back to work, but not to school then. My health waxed and waned, and I needed frequent blood transfusions. By February, I needed my gallbladder and spleen out, and the doctors were a bit apprehen-sive about putting me through surgery but afraid that I wouldn't improve without it. Preparing my family for both good and bad outcomes was difficult to say the least. Dan couldn't talk about it at all. When I woke up from the anesthesia, it was my dad who spoke these words to me: "Jesus is with you, honey." He later told me he had accepted Christ as his Lord and Savior some time ago. I recovered and did fairly well with the occa-sional blood transfusion.

I continued to work full time in labor and delivery. One particular day, it was unusually quiet in the department, as we had no one in labor. All that was scheduled was a non-stress test for a woman pregnant with her first child at age thirty-nine. As I greeted her and settled her on the monitor, I asked the litany of questions required. Her answer to, "Do you have any other children?" elicited a response I didn't expect. She told me how the Lord had blessed her and her husband with two adopted children, a two-and-a-half-year-old son and a four-teen-month-old daughter. Without thinking, I blurted out, "Are you a Christian?" I was so excited to meet another Christian that I talked nonstop the entire time she was there. When she came in the following week, I was waiting for her. Only this time the monitor showed the baby was having some difficulty, so her doctor planned a C-section for later that day. Silly as it may sound, I was overjoyed to be with her and her husband while they awaited the birth of their baby. As I prepped her abdomen for surgery, I heard myself singing, "This is the day the Lord has made." It surprised even me, but later they both told me that had been a huge blessing to them. It's not often that there is time to visit patients after they've delivered, but I felt compelled a couple of days later to visit my new friend. She was tearful and didn't know why. Explaining the hormonal shifts after delivery, I put my arm around her, hugged her, and assured her that what she was feeling is normal. She was discharged the next day, and I didn't expect to see her again.

The following day I received a call from the hospital operator saying that a woman on the phone wanted to talk with a nurse in labor and delivery named Gloria and if I would speak with her. I took the call in a private room, surprised that she'd called, but sure it was about breast-feeding or something related to the birth.

"Something is terribly wrong!" she blurted to my greeting. Through many tears she told me that the pediatrician had heard a heart murmur in the baby and wanted him checked by a specialist before he was taken home. They had stopped at the cardiologist's on the way home, and she had immediately admitted the baby to another hospital with a severe heart defect. An expletive escaped from my undisciplined mouth, and I could have fallen off the face of the earth with embarrassment.

After work for the next few weeks, I took her to the hospital to visit her baby during the day. Three weeks later they took their son to New York City for open-heart surgery, one of many that would be needed. Unfortunately Christopher didn't make it through the next twelve hours post-op. Devastated, they returned home, and the grieving began in earnest.

We walked side by side through the tough times and became the best of friends. She later told me that my expletive expressed exactly how she felt at that moment. Who knew? Her name is Doris, and to this day she is one of my dearest friends.

She often invited me along when she went north to visit her mom. Mabel and I hit it off right away. She was a quilter but had never entered anything into the New York State Fair. I had, so I instructed her on how to enter her very beautiful quilts. She won first place most of the time and taught me how to improve my quilting skills.

Mabel had quite a sense of humor and often acted like I was her favorite whenever Doris and I came to visit. One particular day she greeted us at the door and nodded a courteous hello to Doris but put both of her hands on my face and said, "There's my darling girl." Doris acted offended but really enjoyed the game her mom played. The last time I saw Mabel before she died was at the airport when she was heading to Florida for the winter. She was in her mid–eighties and wheelchair bound. She needed the restroom, so I took her, and when we came out, I ran with her wheelchair through the concourse with her laughing like a young girl. What joy! Her parting gift to me was a queen-sized quilt she had pieced, appliquéd, and hand quilted. I think of her often whenever I look at that quilt and what a gift she was to me in her final years. She really mothered me in a way I didn't know I needed.

Doris and my relationship continued to grow. There wasn't much we didn't know about each other. She had no sisters and felt like God had provided her one in me. Though I had two sisters, one was close, but the other was very critical of me. One weekend we went to a retreat in Fredonia, New York where Patsy Clairmont was the speaker. One of the things she said that resonated with both Doris and me was, "If you're experiencing anger, you're suppressing fear. If you're experiencing fear, you're suppressing anger." Doris and I both pondered that during some free time. She had been having panic attacks and felt angry all the time while I was fearful all the time. Anger wasn't something I liked in Dan or in anyone. The expression of anger scared me a lot. I began to realize I was afraid of not being good enough, doing enough, anyone who didn't like me for whatever reason, making a mistake, being wrong, and being left alone. "But what was I angry about?" I asked myself. "Maybe being abandoned as a child by my family? Or being sexually abused? Or not feeling valued?" I didn't know then.

# CHAPTER 8

A few months later my dad had another heart attack and wasn't expected to survive his stay in ICU. A week later he was transferred to a medical floor to be kept comfortable until he died. Two weeks later he was still alive, able to sit up and eat and even walk around some. My mother refused to take him home from the hospital to care for him. Dan and I prayed with our four children and all decided grandpa could come live with us until he died. My sewing room was changed into a mini-hospital room, and we told dad he was only staying with us until he was well enough to go home. He enjoyed being with our family, and Dan was amazing in the way he helped dad with his physical care. He did fairly well for about a month and then began to slip away. One evening about a week before he died, he asked me if I thought he was going to live or die. "I don't know, Dad, but my question to you is: are you ready?"

He thought for a long time and then said, "For the first time in my life, I'm not afraid. For years I've have had this recurring dream that a casket with people hanging out of it is following me down a hill as I'm running, and they're just missing grabbing onto me. Since I asked Jesus into my heart, I haven't had that dream. If it's time, I'm ready." On June 19th, 1979, I was sitting with my dad as he slipped in and out of consciousness when my two youngest boys asked me to tuck them into bed and pray with them. Reluctant to leave dad, I went upstairs.

When I asked them what they wanted specific prayer for, one of them said, "We want to ask Jesus to come get grandpa and take him to heaven so he doesn't hurt anymore." That's exactly what we prayed, and I then asked Dan to go get my mother as I didn't think dad had much longer. She was so drunk he couldn't rouse her so he came back to be with me. By then dad was home with Jesus, so Dan went back and brought her back quite incoherent, but the scene over my dad's body made me want to hit her.

The first coherent thing she said was, "Where's the money he had?" Really, Mom? Dan eventually took her home, and we made the immediate arrangements with the funeral director. Dad had no life insurance, so Dan and I took out a loan to pay for the funeral. We asked my siblings to help some, but no one could at that time.

The next day I found Pat, then nine, sitting on the back porch crying. Asking him if he were okay, he replied, "I'm going to miss grandpa, Mom, but do you know what I think?"

"No, Honey, what are you thinking? "

"I'm thinking that God must really love us a lot to answer our prayers so fast." I hugged him and told him that God did indeed love us a lot. The next evening, Mike, age eleven, snuggled up to me on the couch and wanted to know when grandpa had given his heart to Jesus. I told him, and he asked if he could have his grandpa's Bible.

"I think grandpa would like that, Honey," I said.

"Mom, I'd like to ask Jesus into my heart right now." With tears of joy, I led my boy in the prayer of salvation and silently thanked God for his grace once again. In October of that same year, Pat prayed to receive Christ at a children's program at a church in our community.

One weekend that same October, a friend of mine from work invited our family to attend her church to hear a group called "Free Spirit." Dan was off on weekends and really had no excuse, so he agreed to go. I had an ulterior motive as he often came home after work complaining about some "puke" he'd arrested. It was during the late seventies when the sex and drug revolution was in full swing. I was concerned as our two oldest kids were approaching that age, and I wanted him to see that there were other late teens and young adults with good values and morals.

He agreed very reluctantly to go, probably more to shut me up than from desire. About 5 AM we had one of the best times of intimacy we had ever had, and afterward Dan asked me what I was learning in all the Bible studies I was attending. I silently prayed for the right words as I didn't want anything I said to deter him from joining the family that morning at church. So I said, "What I'm learning Dan, is the man is the head of his household and responsible before God for his wife and children.

It doesn't matter how spiritual the mother is; the children's relationship with God will parallel their father's, and it hurts me to see you not take that responsibility." He didn't say anything and was very quiet before we left. As with Marriage Encounter he drove "code red" with the other foot on the brake.

When we arrived at the church, the pastor greeted us at the door. I knew him; his wife had had a baby a few weeks before, and I cared for them. Everyone took off their coats except Dan, and the pastor himself ushered us to the front of the sanctuary to the second row. Yikes, Dan liked the very back, but he sat, and we took up the whole row as we had invited friends and their teens to join us. Dan wrapped his jacket around the front of him, folded his arms across his chest, and stared straight ahead. The group sang a few songs, and then there was a puppet show for the kids about salvation. The pastor spoke a few words, and the group members each gave a testimony of how God had delivered them from drugs, alcohol, promiscuity, and so on. Dan had taken his jacket off by this time and was listening intently. After a few more songs the pastor said, "If there is anyone here who doesn't know what his relationship with the Lord Jesus Christ is, I invite him/her to come forward for prayer." Dan didn't move. I selfishly didn't want him to get up, storm out, or make a scene at this point. Then the pastor said, "Come on men, you're the heads of your household and responsible before God for your wife and children." Dan bolted to the front and gave his heart and life to Jesus Christ.

Later he told me he didn't even remember going up front. "It's like two big ole angels picked me up and took me up there," he said with tears streaming down his cheeks. We cried and laughed together all afternoon, and he shared that he had never felt so peaceful. "I was scared to even go into that church, Gloria. In parochial school it was drummed into my head that if I ever went into a Protestant church, I'd go straight to hell. You have no idea how frightened I was." Within a couple of months, our whole family was saved, and we were baptized together.

My sister Jan came to visit and was curious about our new faith in Christ. Very involved in Wiccan, she couldn't imagine what we found so awesome about God, but she peppered me with many questions. She began to realize that Wiccan didn't give her the peace that she saw in us, and after several nights of conversations until the wee hours of the morning, she gave her heart to Christ and has served him since. One by one my siblings came to Christ as did most of their children. Each of them is different in his or her walk, but all love and worship the same Heavenly Father.

# CHAPTER 9

C ontent with my job and feeling well, I was surprised to receive a call from the director of nursing asking me to come to her office. She wanted to know if I was interested in reentering the nurse practitioner program. "I'll have to pray about it and discuss it with my husband," I answered. Dan was very agreeable, and through prayer I knew that God had reopened that door.

Wondering which doctor I could ask to be my preceptor (a mentor who takes responsibility for providing experiences for learning), I was very surprised when one of my favorites came into the department and said, "I heard you were going into the NP program, and I'd be honored to be your preceptor." Only God! I began the program the next week, and my health remained stable throughout.

Towards the end, I began having issues with my remaining ovary, and it needed to be removed. The surgery went well, but the recovery was tumultuous. I'd had trouble lifting my right leg after the surgery but didn't think much of it. It didn't improve, and I was getting paler and paler, plus I had an infection in my incision. The surgeon claimed I was hemolyzing (a result of my autoimmune antibody), and the oncologist said I was bleeding internally. A CAT scan revealed a large blood clot in my abdomen that required another surgery and blood transfusions. The muscle that controls lifting of my leg was enmeshed with blood clot explaining the inability to raise it. The surgery went well but complications required a five-week hospitalization, multiple antibiotics, and no definite answers as to the outcome. Many nights I lay awake searching for answers from God.

One particular night, as I lay awake in the hospital asking God "why," I heard in my spirit that the Father would be glorified. I sort of dismissed it as I wasn't sure how or if I'd even heard right. A deacon from our church visited me the next day. He was a young man and seemed exceptionally excited that day. He couldn't wait to tell me that God had impressed on him to read to me from John 9. In it the disciples were questioning Jesus about a blind man, asking him who sinned, this man or his parents such that he was born blind. Jesus answered, "Neither this man nor his parents sinned," said Jesus, "but this happened so that the work of God might be displayed in his life"(John 9:3). God is so good. He confirmed what I had heard in the night.

A few weeks later when things weren't progressing as the doctors had hoped, it was decided I needed nutrition because I hadn't eaten since before the surgery. A relatively new and risky procedure then, I was scared but decided I had nothing to lose. Naked from the waist up, my face covered, feeling vulnerable, crying, and with a catheter being put into the subclavian vein in my chest wall, I prayed Job 13:15: "Though you slay me; still I will trust You."

Somehow I knew everything would be okay. My daughter had been away for the weekend, and when she visited, she said Ken had asked her to marry him, and she had accepted. They wanted to get married in three months as he was in the service and needed to take leave then. She also wanted me to make her wedding gown. Nutrition was what I needed, and within ten days, all systems were working and I was discharged, weak but able to function.

Kelly and I had a wonderful time together planning her wedding and laughing as we did multiple fittings of her gown. I had never made a wedding gown before and because it was her desire for me to do so, I felt honored and tackled it with determination wanting it to be everything she dreamed; simple but elegant.

Enjoying the process

As Dan and I walked her down the aisle, we looked at each other and both wondered where the years had gone. *Wasn't she just an infant two weeks ago?* She and Ken left at 10 PM the same night for Oklahoma. Sadness filled our home for the next two weeks. Often, I'd find Pat sulking in the family room because he missed his sister so much; we all did. It felt more like a funeral than a wedding. We travelled to Oklahoma to visit a few times, driving round the clock as our schedules allowed.

Ken and Kelly wanted children right away, and she was soon pregnant only to lose the baby at fourteen weeks. A few months later she was pregnant again, and I began sewing the crib ensemble plus anything else I could think of. In November of 1983, our oldest son graduated from Navy boot camp the day after Thanksgiving. Kelly and I talked the day before and everything was fine. We travelled all day on Thanksgiving with our two youngest boys.

We hadn't told anyone where we were staying as all of our family was accounted for. The motel we stayed in was substandard, so we checked out the morning of graduation and spent the day with Danny. Intending to spend another night in Chicago and drive home the next day, we were surprised to hear our two boys say that they wanted to go home, not stay in another motel, so we did, thankfully.

Arriving home at 11AM, I picked up the messages on the phone and several panicked ones from a family friend alarmed me. When I finally got in touch with her, she struggled to tell me what was going on. Kelly's baby was dead. I called Ken to find out what was going on. He told me that the baby had been fine at the Wednesday appointment but hadn't moved since

Thanksgiving. An ultrasound revealed no heartbeat, so she was being induced.

"Do you want me to come," I asked.

"Mom, the baby is dead," he stammered.

"I want to be there for you both so is it okay if I come?" With what sounded like relief, he assured me he did. Four planes and eight hours later, I arrived in Oklahoma, not sure who was picking me up at the airport, or if the military personnel would even let me in the labor room with them. It was nearly midnight when I got to the hospital, praying all the way that I would be allowed to be with my daughter. The nurses were great and ushered me into her room. She hadn't been told I was coming, so sobbed when she saw me. She had been being induced for almost sixteen hours without any progress and was exhausted. The doctor came into the room to examine her and started talking to me. He was emotionally involved in their plight as his wife had lost a baby the same time Kelly had lost her first child and was expecting again. We talked about Kelly's progress, and he seemed to be perplexed as he pondered his next move. He even asked me what I thought as he knew I had a lot of experience as a labor and delivery nurse. I suggested rest and a restart in the morning to which he agreed. Kelly was given a sedative, and Ken and I stayed until she was almost asleep.

We left with adamant instructions to the staff that when she awoke, we were to be called even if she wasn't laboring. We hadn't slept for more than a few hours when the call came at 4 AM. We hurried to the hospital, and she was indeed laboring.

The doctor arrived about 5, and she had progressed so much, he took Ken to change his clothes for delivery. While they were gone, Kelly said, "Mom, the baby's coming." Going into automatic mode, I looked to see if she was right, when Daniel Walter came into his grandma's hands rapidly. I shook him slightly and demanded that he breathe. My head knew the truth, but my heart hadn't accepted it yet. The nurses lovingly foot printed Daniel, and I took pictures to help his parents grieve. I stayed a week and then had to get home for work.

As soon as I stepped off the plane, I fell into Dan's arms, and our grief began in earnest. Until then, I'd had no idea how much grandparents grieve, not only about death, but family estrangement, divorce among their children, illness, suicide, murder, accidents, and so much more. At work I began to address not only the parents when they suffered a loss, but the grandparents as well. God did teach me much about Himself though Daniel's death.

Two months later, on New Year's Eve, the pastor of the church Ken and Kelly attended challenged everyone to "shamelessly storm heaven for an answer to prayer in 1984." He encouraged anyone willing to do that to meet with him and his wife so they could join in praying. They took the challenge and prayed for a healthy baby in 1984. By mid-spring, Kelly was pregnant, excited yet very apprehensive. I think she held her breath though most of the pregnancy, especially up to the point Daniel had been born. They had picked out the names Alexander James and Katherine Victoria.

On the way home from work sometime later, Ken heard the name Zachary in his spirit, and when he got home, asked Kelly what she thought of that name. "It's a fine name, but if we have a boy, his name is Alexander James." While shopping at a mall one weekend, Kelly went into a baby store and thumbed through a book of baby names. She looked up Zachary and when she discovered it meant "Jehovah has remembered," she ran to the computer store where Ken was to tell him. They both rejoiced and when their baby boy was born December 10, 1984, he was named Zachary Andrew. Jehovah had remembered. Nineteen months later they had their Katherine Victoria and four years after that, Emily Gloria was born. They pray for and rejoice in their children every day as do I.

# CHAPTER 10

n June of 1986, a few of my co-workers wanted to know more about the God I served as did a long-time friend. After four of them had accepted Christ as their Lord and Savior, I heard the Lord speak to my spirit: "Gloria, you can't leave these new believers on their own; I want you to teach them."

"Not me, Lord, You know I don't even like to teach even new nurses their jobs. I don't have the patience."

"Do you trust me Gloria?"

What was I going to say to the One who died for me? "No." "Okay Lord, I'm really going to need your help." The first person who was interested in a Bible study was my long-time friend and neighbor. So we planned a date, and I showed up at her house with every reference book I owned. We started with the basics, and when I left, I felt exhilarated at having been obedient.

The following week she asked if she could bring a friend, and her friend prayed with us to receive Christ that evening. God was surely at work in all of our lives. The friend wanted to bring another friend, and it wasn't long before we had a group of eight to ten each week. Not all were believers, but all did eventually bow their knees and hearts to Jesus Christ. There were times when I'd show up to Bible study totally unprepared, and all went well. Other times, the Holy Spirit changed the topic entirely but graced us with exactly what was needed that particular evening. We were all on a huge learning curve, and those years were some of the best. Each woman eventually answered a call to a separate ministry and is still serving today.

During the summer each year a group of my friends and I went to a Christian camp in the Adirondacks. My friend and mentor led and taught the retreat. She started asking me to do a devotional and then the next year one of the teachings. I told her I couldn't do that, and her response was, "That's right. You can't," reminding me that it was God at work in me. A few summers later, as I drove home from the weekend retreat, I heard the Spirit within me say that I would be teaching the whole retreat in the next few years. Again, I doubted but said nothing to anyone.

The next year my mentor and I drove the two-hour trip together. As we neared the camp, she told me that she felt the Lord telling her this would be the last year she'd be leading.

All I said was, "I know."

"What," she exclaimed. "I've been very apprehensive about telling you this for almost six months." I explained what I had heard the year before, and we both rejoiced in God's goodness. We had a wonderful weekend, and for the next five years I led and taught that particular retreat.

One spring, I was asked to do a retreat for the ladies in my church. I had done other ones for other churches but never my own. I was frightened. As I prayed, I felt the Lord telling me to say yes. I really didn't want to, but in the next breath, I asked what topic they wanted me to do. "Whatever the Lord puts on your heart," was the reply. Yikes!

During prayer once again I heard the Lord instruct me to teach on the Proverbs 31 woman. "You have got to be kidding, Lord. Single women think it doesn't apply, and married women think it is too hard."

He said, "You meditate on those twenty-one verses for the next thirty days, and I'll give you what you need." I read and struggled over those verses for a month, sometimes pacing as I sought His answers to my questions. He gave me insight like I'd never experienced. The retreat went well, and once again God had been faithful.

Another time I was doing a retreat about an hour and a half from home. I had asked two friends to attend the retreat—one to pray throughout and the other to critique the content. Doris was an educator, and I really wasn't sure if the content flowed. They both sat where I could see them as I spoke. Just before the worship was to begin, I was setting up the podium with my Bible and my notes. What notes? I couldn't find them anywhere. It was then I realized I had taken them to work with me the night before to review and had left them on the counter at home instead of packing them. Panic set in as I tried to figure out what I was going to do. Some of the ladies had driven miles to get there so I couldn't cancel. There wasn't time to call Dan to bring them. I sat down next to Doris and prayed fervently, not telling her what had happened. The last worship song we sang just before I was to speak was "Have Thine Own Way, Lord." The last line of the chorus is, "While I am waiting, yielded and still." I felt anything but yielded and still. As I walked to the podium I prayed God would show up in a big way. The topic was communication, and the only scripture I could remember from my many pages of notes was James 1:19: "Be quick to listen, slow to speak and slow to anger." As I spoke I flipped an empty sheet of paper over and over. I spoke on listening for over an hour. When I finished I asked Doris what she thought. "I got so caught up in what you were saying that I forgot to critique the content."

"I forgot my notes," I confessed.

"But you kept flipping a sheet of paper," she said.

"Yes, a blank one." We were both so excited about what God had done that it was the wee hours of the morning before either of us went to sleep. Saturday morning I spoke on speaking, and the afternoon session was on anger, all without my notes. God is so good.

# CHAPTER 11

M eanwhile, my mother was living in a senior apartment complex and drunk most of the time. Many were the calls I received in the late evening or wee hours of the morning that she had fallen and was on her way to the hospital by ambulance. The first few times I went immediately, but watching her go through withdrawal for three days was something I soon tired of.

After that I waited for several days before I'd go see her, and it was usually after a social worker had called to talk about post-hospitalization care. Dan and I made arrangements for her to go through several rehabilitation programs, which helped for limited periods of time. Her apartment was a mess as she wasn't motivated to clean it. Her day consisted of sitting in a recliner, watching TV with a glass full of vodka without ice. She thought if it looked like water, we would think it was water. She drank between 64 and 128 ounces of gin or vodka every couple of days. She'd call the liquor store and have it delivered.

One afternoon a young man called me to say he'd just arrived at my mother's and couldn't wake her to get paid for her booze. My response: "keep trying or take it back." I know that sounds callous, but I had had about enough. After one hospitalization, mom was told she couldn't live alone anymore. She was beside herself as she hadn't turned seventy yet. I told her I'd go to bat for her one more time on several conditions: no more drinking, regular counseling sessions, AA meetings. "One more alcohol related hospitalization, mom, and your apartment will be gone." She did well for a little over a year. We had a huge party for her to celebrate one year of sobriety.

About three months later she was drinking again. At midnight one night that I was working, Dan called me to say mom was on her way to the hospital I worked in because she had fallen again and one of her neighbors had called an ambulance. "Not here," I screamed, "have someone divert the ambulance to the hospital she usually goes to. They have her records there." My work place was the only place mom hadn't tainted. I know this sounds selfish, but I didn't want to have to deal with her issues with my colleagues. She arrived in the ER as I was in a small room praying for grace. To make a long story short, she had liver failure with brain toxicity and wasn't expected to live. I called all my siblings who came from around the country, signed the DNR, and was ashamed for my attitude. My siblings were supportive and understood. Half of them didn't want to be there either. Three days later she woke up and wanted to know where her &*^*# teeth were.

That day I received a call from the manager of her apartment complex saying she couldn't live there alone anymore as many of the seniors in her building were trying to care for her to their own detriment. Now the pressure was off me for following through on my earlier promise should she resume drinking. The doctor caring for her talked with all of us and suggested an adult home with which he often was involved. We visited and decided it would be a safe place for her, and the administrator told me she would not be able to drink while there. Mom was not happy but had no choice at that point. My siblings went back to their respective homes and families while Dan and I tried to settle her into her new room. There were twenty-five other residents, and she'd have regular meals and activities. Her daily calls to me were often complaining about some annoyance, and she let me know repeatedly how unhappy she was to be there.

"Mom, do you remember when you put us all in the orphanage to keep us safe because you couldn't keep a roof over our heads?"

"Yes," she replied sheepishly.

"Did you do it to hurt us?"

"No."

"This isn't to hurt you either but to keep you safe and hopefully not falling as much." I know she didn't like that line of reasoning, but she didn't argue. Many times mom came up with more ideas about how she could now live on her own. She could usually be calmed down and agreed to stay where she was.

# CHAPTER 12

For the next ten years my health was fairly stable with periods of chemo and a few blood transfusions. One afternoon Dan and I were both riding in the car when I began to complain about a professor I had been taking a class from.

"I think I'll drop the course. I'm tired and not feeling that great," I announced.

"You're not dropping it because of your health. You're dropping it because you're not sure you'll get an A. When are you going to stop jumping through hoops for your dad?"

I dawned on me that was exactly what I was doing. I finished the course with a B. Dan and I went out to dinner to celebrate my freedom. I received straight A grades for each course after that but knew I didn't have to, and it made all the difference.

The New York State Fair is a highlight of the summer for most Central New Yorkers. We decided to take our daughter Kelly and her children to the fair one afternoon. I was driving, and we stopped at the pharmacy for Dan to pick up a prescription for himself. He had been injured in the police car and still had a fair amount of pain. The sun was shining brightly, and there was low humidity and a slight breeze. It couldn't have been a nicer day when I turned to talk to Kelly in the back seat and my left arm went numb and fell off the steering wheel. I couldn't move it. When I tried to talk my speech was garbled. Kelly thought I was fooling around but when she saw the fear in my eyes, she ran into the pharmacy to get Dan. We did not get to the fair that day; I went to the hospital. After a battery of tests it was determined I'd had a mini-stroke. We were all very frightened. A few days later as I was praying about all that had happened, I heard the LORD say I needed to deal with some unresolved issues stemming from my childhood.

"Not me Lord. I'm fine," I blurted.

"Let Me help you to heal so you can live a full life," He whispered gently.

"Okay Lord, but this really scares me. No one in our family has ever needed a shrink!" When I told Dan, he blanched, scared of the very idea. His dad had been to psychiatrists and in a mental institution most of his life. I think he was afraid that was going to happen to me.

"Just let me work some stuff out, Dan. Apparently it's affecting me more than I think." I found a Christian counselor and started weekly sessions. At first it seemed like a waste of time and money, but the deeper we got into some of my stuff, the more I realized it really affected my entire being. I was angry about a number of things to the point that it also spilled over into all of my relationships. Dan was skeptical but very supportive, and when I finally did begin to realize that I didn't have to be all things to all people at all times and could learn to say the word "no," I was much calmer and less intense. I was angry with my abuser for affecting my relationship with Dan. I'd jump if Dan touched me in certain ways, and he kept telling me he wasn't going to hurt me. "It's not you, Dan. I can't help it; it's almost instinctive, but I'll try to learn to do better."

Later that year we were at the wedding of our son Patrick's friend. Pat was the best man, so he and his wife Holly were seated at the head table. Our son Mike and his wife MaryKay were seated at a table with Dan and me along with four or five octogenarians during the reception. After dinner Mike and his wife left, but Dan and I stayed for a while. I have always loved older people, so I began talking with our tablemates. Recognizing the name of the church, I asked if this was the same one I had attended as a child.

"Yes," said one of the ladies excitedly. "After many years we outgrew the little church you attended. We've only been in this one a few years."

"I was in foster care with a family who attended the other one," I said.

"What was the family's name?"

I told her but wasn't prepared for her response.

"She died several years ago, but he just died a year or so ago. What a pillar of the church he was," she announced proudly.

Everything from the core of my being wanted to stand in the middle of the table and tell them all what their "pillar of the church" had done to me when I was eleven years old. I knew it would only hurt them, and so I couldn't do it, but I gave Dan the signal that I wanted to leave. We graciously said our good-byes and left. I barely made it to the car before bursting into wracking sobs. Dan held me close, trying to understand what had happened. As I sobbed, I felt like all the pain of the abuse was leaving my soul. I now believe that a large chunk of the wall around my heart came crashing down that day. I thank my God that happened as the retelling of this story is no longer painful, but merely a matter of fact. I had forgiven my perpetrator, and maybe he had repented and been forgiven by God too. It isn't for me to judge.

One of my favorite pictures of me as a 4 year old is with a wicker doll carriage in front of a small tree in our yard.

I began to want a doll and a wicker baby carriage. Pretty silly for a fifty year old, I thought. Dan was all for it and went on a quest to find exactly what I wanted. We searched every antique shop across New York State to no avail.

That fall, we flew to Oregon to visit our friends Sally Stuart and Norm Wilson. Sally likes to go antiquing so she took us to some really nice antique shops. One was a three-story co-op, and while I was on the third floor looking at old lace and other things, Dan was on the lower level hunting for a wicker doll carriage.

Startled to hear him calling me quite loudly, I hurried to him, thinking maybe something else might be wrong as he'd been having some heart issues. He had found the most perfect white, wicker doll carriage and was so excited he was yelling. It was in perfect condition but came with a ratty doll that had definitely been mistreated by its previous owner. When we paid for the carriage I told the cashier that I didn't want the doll. She informed me it came with the carriage. So I took it. We travelled by train to Los Angeles, California to see our son Danny and his wife. While there Dan bought me a beautiful porcelain Gorham doll to go with the carriage. He was thrilled to give it to me for my birthday. We shipped everything home, and I couldn't wait to reassemble the carriage and have my new doll in it so it would be just the way I'd remembered.

My three-year-old granddaughter Katie visited overnight a few weeks later and wanted to play with both dolls. Selfishly I let her play with the ratty one but not the new one. To clarify she asked, "I no toucha that baby but this baby okay, right Grammy?"

"Yes," I answered feeling possessive and ashamed. She obeyed with no problem, but I began to be convicted about my behavior. One afternoon while Dan napped, I heard the Lord tell me to pick up the ratty doll and really look at it. She had a cloth body, hair cut right down to stubble, nail polish on one hand and not the other, and her face had been scribbled with magic marker with one eye open and the other stuck shut. I took her into the kitchen and washed off the magic marker and opened the stuck eye, which just kept getting stuck. She also had a cry mechanism in her that, when tipped forward, was supposed to make a crying sound. Compelled, I went into the sewing room and found a pair of pink preemie booties and put them on her feet. Soon I was making her new white bloomers, a slip, and a fancy pink dress. Later that week I took her to a doll shop, had her crier fixed, her eye unstuck permanently, and bought a new wig. I named her Hannah Grace.

Little by little God began to show me what he had done for me through that ratty old doll. He had washed me clean, put warm socks on my cold feet, covered my sexual abuse with pure white, and dressed me in new garments. He also opened both my eyes to see more clearly, gave me new hair after chemo, and added a new name that I will know when I meet Him face to face. He had made me beautiful even though I had been abused and marred. I felt new inside as well. I now have a theory—not a proven fact, just a theory—that if people don't deal with their "stuff" by the time they're fifty they wind up isolating and becoming even more miserable. There's nothing magical about fifty; it could be forty or sixty, but a time comes when we don't have the energy to keep all our stuff at bay, and it crops up unexpectedly and usually inappropriately. I am so grateful that God showed me the way to healing.

Our whole family at Dan's surprise 60th birthday party

# CHAPTER 13

I finally finished my degree in nursing in 1990, six months before my fiftieth birthday. Because I had a high GPA, the university encouraged me to go on for a master's degree. It had taken thirteen years of consistent work to finish the BSN, so I was undecided. My health had waxed and waned, and remissions were less than a year before I needed more chemo. I had been told that when this particular drug didn't work anymore, there weren't any other effective drugs to use. I needed to cut back on all the activities I was involved in and heard the Lord tell me in prayer one day to not go on for a master's degree but to go on for the Master. Grateful for His direction, I declined the university's offer.

Dan was injured when he was rear-ended by a drunk driver, sustaining permanent nerve damage in his neck even after surgery. Despite this, we had bought a twenty-four-foot cabin cruiser that we towed to Kingston, Ontario and launched at the beginning of the Rideau Canal. We then travelled through forty locks to Ottawa, Canada. The view throughout the entire trip each year was pristine. Most of the locks were hand-turned by two men. Every other night we'd dock on the lock and enjoy nature without electricity or computers or phones.

Once we passed Smith Falls, all sense of civilization waned, and the peace we both experienced was unimaginable. The opposite nights we'd stay in a marina where we could plug into shore power, take showers, and get fuel. Often on those trips, God would give me everything I needed for the upcoming retreat I did the third week in August each year. Even though Dan had chronic pain in his right arm from the injury, he rarely complained. Usually by the end of most days he had to stop using his arm at all. We thoroughly enjoyed taking that trip each year.

A couple of years we took our oldest grandson Zak along with us. One particular year when he was nine, we took our usual trip and another couple with a boat went with us. They had never been on the Rideau Canal and loved the trip and really enjoyed Zak.

On a beautiful sunny morning we left the lock where we had stayed the night. The first set of locks we encountered was at Jones Falls, a series of four locks. My job whenever we approached a lock was to grab the bowline and be ready to jump off onto the dock to tie up the front of the boat while Dan used the engines to bring the back in so I could tie up the stern line. I was ready to jump when the next thing I remembered was waking up on the dock. Dan said I fell straight off and landed on my face with my head bouncing twice before I was still. He thought for sure I was dead and had a lot of trouble getting the boat into the dock by himself. Zak was scared as were our friends. A doctor was standing on the dock and came to see if I was okay, but her husband stopped her and they walked away. Because we were Americans, they were afraid we'd sue them. Dan was beside himself, and Zak was traumatized. The nearest hospital was over two hours away by car. I had a cut the full length of my right eyelid, so we taped the edges together with strips of the sticky part of a Band-Aid and except for a pounding headache, I seemed to be okay, so I again took my position at the bowline as we traveled eight hours to get to the next marina.

Once there, my headache was so bad that Dan inquired about the nearest hospital and whether or not we could get a cab. Our friends were willing to care for Zak who by this time, seemed to be okay. The guy working at the marina told us he would be off work in less than an hour and if we could wait, he'd be willing to take us to a hospital. What a blessing. After a CT scan of my head and some pain meds, I was released. Back at the marina, I went right to bed, and Dan cared for Zak the rest of the evening.

The headaches continued, so I saw my regular doctor once we got back home. He ordered an MRI of my head, which showed I had a brain tumor. "Not my brain, Lord!" I cried. "Not my brain!" I was told the tumor could be benign, malignant, or an aneurysm. I didn't think any of them was a particularly good choice. After several specialists looked at the films, the diagnosis was a benign tumor in the temporal lobe and that my earlier episode at the pharmacy and the fact that I had no recollection of falling off the boat determined that I had had an incomplete seizure and a full blown one from this tumor.

My driver's license was temporarily suspended for six months, and every year after for ten years the DMV sent me paperwork to fill out determining whether or not I could continue to drive. Thankfully I never had another seizure. It seemed now that every part of my body, including my brain, had some malady. God has used every situation to draw me closer to Him, and I praise Him for it.

One day a young fifteen-year-old girl that I had taught in Sunday school called and asked me if I would mentor her. She came from a healthy family, and I couldn't imagine how I could do an adequate job. We met weekly throughout her high school years and became good friends as well despite the thirty-five-plus year age difference. The twenty year old inside of me related well to her young years. We kept in touch through her college years as well. She'd call with various issues relating to studies, boys, girls, and college life. During her senior year she had been dating a young man named Greg. She was bringing him home on school break to introduce him to her parents. "Gloria, we want to take you out to dinner while we're home, and I need your opinion about Greg."

"Really, why do you want my opinion?"

"It's important to me," she said. We met at a favorite restaurant and talked for three hours. Greg was and is a delightful young man and seemed to be a perfect match for Hilary. "So what do you think?" she asked when we were alone.

"I think if you don't marry him, I will."

Hilary laughed right out loud and responded, "But you're already married!"

They married a couple of years later and asked me to be the matron of honor. "Really, Hil, do you really want a sixty-plus year old in your wedding party? I don't want you looking at your wedding pictures in ten years and wondering what you were thinking."

"I want people standing up for our wedding who I know will support our marriage, and I'd be honored if you would."

"I will, and it's a great privilege to do so." We have remained good friends since. She has gone on to get a second degree in nursing, had two babies, and just finished a master's program as an oncology and palliative care nurse practitioner. I have been privileged to attend most of her graduations and couldn't be prouder of her. Greg is a wonderful husband, father, and pastor.

# CHAPTER 14

D an and I made the decision to sell the boat as it was beginning to be too much for him to handle with his chronic pain. A few years later we bought a Bounder motor home.

Proud owners

Our children were all married to believers by then, and Dan was retired. We traveled on weekends and on my vacations.

We also joined a Bounder camping group. Each couple owned a Bounder, and we camped together many times. We met many wonderful campers and became especially good friends with a couple who lived about ten miles from us. The four of us often met for dinner somewhere in the off season as well.

Our most memorable trip was with our good friends and two other couples that we hooked up with in Arizona and California. We then spent a few weeks in Santa Barbara. We had some issues with our rig in California and had to stay in a motel for a few days. Eventually we left with one of the couples and toured Arizona. When they went their way, we decided to head home. We had a book titled *See America Coast to Coast; Stay Free Every Night*. We looked it over and decided to take the challenge to see if we could get back to New York without paying for camping overnight. It wasn't a money issue; it was a challenge. We had a blast finding Walmarts, rest areas, truck stops, and Cracker Barrel restaurants to park overnight.

Having just come through some rather nasty weather in the Rockies, we were happy to be in Oklahoma and stopped in a rest area for the night. When Dan turned off the motor home, the car lights didn't go off like they should. He fiddled with a bunch of stuff to try and fix the problem to no avail. We finally had to call our roadside assistance plan for help. A man from a garage in Enid, Oklahoma responded and told us we had a breaker switch out and asked us to follow him to the garage. We did. By that time it was getting late. We had already lost an hour going through a time zone and it was also the night to switch to daylight savings time. Dale came out of the shop to tell us he didn't have the part but could get it in the morning. We asked if there was a place we could park overnight. He showed us to a spot, and we settled in to have a light dinner. We also asked if there was a church nearby for us to attend in the morning. He told us about the church he went to and gave us directions. A few minutes later he was knocking on our door. "I just talked with our pastor, and he has invited you to park your rig in the church's parking lot for the night. It'll be quieter and you can plug into power," he said.

"Thank you, and what a blessing!" Dan responded. We had a good night's rest and attended Sunday school and the church service the next morning. Dale was there looking very tired. He'd been up all night getting a tractor trailer out of a sand filled ditch. After church while Dale was on the phone, the pastor's wife spoke with me in the parking lot.

"Did Dale tell you about himself?"

"No."

"He is one of our success stories. The penitentiary is only a few miles from here, and we pick up some of the inmates and bring them to church and disciple them. Dale and his wife were in prison. He came to Jesus, has been released, and is now chairman of our missions board. His wife is coming along. Do you see those three little girls over there playing?"

"Yes, they're darling," I replied.

"The littlest one was born in prison," she said pointing to the child. All three girls were dressed beautifully and seemed very happy. This little church of sixty ministered in a big way to the prisoners and had made a huge difference in many of the inmates' lives. Dale then came to us telling us he couldn't get the part until the next day. Our three-year-old granddaughter Hannah had called and talked to Dan, who she called Bumpa, crying that she missed him and when were we coming home. That's all Dan needed to hear. Now he was in a huge hurry to get home. He asked Dale if we could drive the rig safely home without the part.

"Sure," he said. "There are two switches for that purpose so I'll just change them over, and you can be on your way." We left that afternoon, grateful for the way we had been welcomed by God's family. We talked for most of the afternoon about how amazed we were by the work that little church was doing in and for their community.

On that same trip home, we stopped for the night in a rest area in Missouri. We went to bed fairly early, and Dan wanted the alarm set for 4:30 AM, which I did. About 10:30 PM neither of us was sure we had been to sleep yet but did eventually fall off. The next thing I knew Dan was shaking my shoulder asking me if I was going to get up. "What time is it?"

"About 4:50. I've showered and shaved, taken my meds and am getting ready to eat breakfast," he said.

"Okay, I'll be up in a minute." A few minutes later Dan came into the bathroom and asked me if I knew what time it was.

"No."

"It's 12:30 AM. What time did you set the alarm for?"

"4:30AM like you asked. Did it go off, because I didn't hear it." I said.

"Yes. What do you want to do now?"

"We might as well get going. We're both dressed and awake." So we left and drove the rest of the way home. By the time we got to Buffalo (two hours from home) at 3 PM, I wanted to stop to sleep for an hour or so.

"Just stay awake and talk to me. We're going the rest of the way." It was the longest two hours of my life. But we were home safely, and our little Hannah was elated.

Hannah with her Grammy

Pat, his wife Holly, three-year-old Hannah, and baby Jonah were living with us while they built their home in Cortland. We found out later that even though the rig had plugs for electrical things when we weren't plugged into shore power, clocks just went round and round without stopping or really keeping time. It had eventually hit 4:30 and gone off. So we were both right. We bought a manual clock for further trips!

# CHAPTER 15

In the adult home mom's manipulative behavior escalated even though she wasn't drinking anymore. At this point she decided she was moving out and that I was going to help her accomplish her goal. She insisted I pick her up and take her somewhere to talk privately. I asked my sister Jan to go with me as I was on chemotherapy and knew I didn't have the energy to deal with my mother.

While sitting in the restaurant, my mother explained to my sister and me all the reasons she wanted to move and dictating how we were to help. We tried to help her problem solve some of the difficulties she was having with the staff at the adult home. When she realized we weren't going to help her move, she got angry and belligerent. On the way back to her home, she made some nasty remark to me that I don't even remember, but it set me off and for the first time in my life, I told my mother just how I felt. How she understood me through the choking sobs, I'll never know, but she got the idea I was upset, and she had never seen that in me before. One thing she had drilled into my head when I was growing up was that a child does not speak back to an adult. Sadly, whenever I was with her, I reverted to being a child.

Jan went in with mom and anticipated that she'd have to put the pieces together after my outburst. Mom seemed unaffected and even asked Jan if she wanted to see her new bathing suit.

Jan and I drove to a convenience store parking lot and talked for over an hour. We both needed to debrief. Old childhood issues of inadequacy raised their ugly heads in both of us. Thankfully we had each other.

My usual way of dealing with confrontational episodes is to withdraw and remain distant until it feels safe enough to reengage. Within a few days the Lord spoke to me in prayer when I was asking forgiveness for my behavior and He told me I had it all wrong. Instead of withdrawing, now was the time to draw closer to my mother and not abandon her in my anger. I sure didn't want to hear that, but in obedience went to the adult home to see mom. She, too, was distant and after sitting with her for a while, I left. Gradually we were able to reconnect much sooner than we had in the past.

For over two years I was being nudged in my spirit that it was time to retire. Dan was already retired and wanted to travel more. At age fifty-eight I was afraid to retire. Would we have enough money? Would I be content staying home? Why now when the kids are grown and gone? Would I be bored? All these questions kept me from moving towards retirement. It was getting harder to run (literally) for deliveries, and I hadn't gone to the cafeteria in months for fear I wouldn't make it back in time for an emergency. I was also helping out in an infusion center with the preemie graduates who needed an IV medication through the winter. I'd get off one job at 7:30 AM, grab an hour nap, and head to the other job.

One evening at work I began to feel quite ill. *Just a cold,* I thought. I felt worse as the evening and night progressed. When I left in the morning I went right to the other job thinking I'd be okay. By 11 AM I had a fever with shaking chills. I called the nurse practitioner in my oncologist's office, and she called in a prescription for antibiotics for me. As soon as I picked the drugs up after work, I went home and straight to bed. The next day I didn't even get dressed. The chemo I had been on for over ten years wasn't working anymore, and my doctor wanted to admit me to the bone marrow transplant unit and give me very high doses of the drug without the benefit of a bone marrow transplant. My gut told me not to do it, so I was struggling with that decision as well as not feeling well.

Dan and I had made an appointment with our lawyer for the next day to update our wills, get powers of attorney for each other, and make sure our health care proxies were up to date. During the night I knew my fever was very high but didn't bother taking my temperature. Instead I took a couple of Tylenol and went back to bed.

The morning of our appointment with the lawyer we woke up to a snowstorm, and I could hardly navigate. My fever was over 103. I called the nurse practitioner again, and she ordered me to come right into the office. In the shower I couldn't get warm no matter how hot the water was. By the time I got out and dressed, my fever was up to 104 and almost 105 when I got to the doctor's office. I was admitted almost immediately.

Everything in my body went haywire. I had pneumonia, was hemolyzing, and rapidly deteriorating. My doctor was out of town, and the one covering that day was the same one who would be taking over my care when my doctor left for North Carolina. No one really wanted to do anything until my doctor got back except give me antibiotics and blood transfusions, which they did. After discharge I was to again see my own doctor in the clinic. In the meantime Dan and I began to feel very uncomfortable with the idea of high dose chemo as we had been told three times in one office visit that there was the possibility of a fatal cardio-toxicity associated with the treatment.

It was time to retire, but I was so frightened. I did all the what-ifs and yeah-buts I could think of, asking the same questions over and over again. I called the MD Anderson Hospital in Houston, Texas to speak with a doctor I had consulted with five years earlier. He had given me his home number and asked me to call him anytime I had a question. He happened to be home the evening I called, and when I had told him what was going on, I said, "I just need to know if the high dose chemo is a viable option."

"Sure it's a viable option, but there is so much more you can do before you have to try that one."

"Like what?"

"Like Rituxan," he said, explaining that although it had only been approved for the lymphomas, they were getting great results using it for the autoimmune diseases. "Have your doctor send me a two-year summary of your care, and I'll send him the protocol for this treatment. Or you could come here for it, but it's once a week for four weeks." He also cited some literature that had been written about the drug. I thanked him and said that he'd be hearing from us. Going to Texas was out of the question as we had driven the thirty-six hour trip once already and knew we couldn't do that every week for four weeks. Dan hated to fly.

In the meantime I prayed about retirement. I had six months of sick time after which I wouldn't have a job, and I loved my job. So I told the LORD I'd apply for Social Security disability (because I'd get my full pension if I was on disability), and if it wasn't approved within six months, I'd go back to work. Besides I'd already worked so many years that my pension was at the max anyway. Working longer wasn't going to yield five cents per month more at age sixty-five. Not very spiritual telling God what I'm going to do, but I did, and He honored it anyway. I was approved for Social Security in sixty days. Only God!

Convincing my doctor was another story. When I mentioned that I had called MD Anderson, he was livid. "They can afford to give you tea and cookies when you go there, but this hospital is every bit as current in these matters as they are," he yelled. "Besides, the literature is anecdotal at best."

"Please cancel my bed on the bone marrow transplant unit as I'm not comfortable doing the high dose chemo," I said as calmly as I could at the moment.

"Okay, but I'm not sure if I'll be able to get you another bed anytime soon," he added. He wanted to see me again in three weeks, and I left unhappy but trusting God. The next time I had an appointment he was friendly and asked me when I wanted to start the Rituxan.

"What changed your mind?" I asked.

"Well I read the article and found it was written by a friend of mine, so I called him," he answered rather sheepishly. "And I'm convinced after speaking with him that there is a lot of promise in using this drug not only for you, but for others in similar situations."

"Oh, so because a friend of yours wrote the article it now has validity," I replied snidely.

"So when do you want to start the new treatment?" he asked.

"As soon as possible." With that he talked to the nurse practitioner about who else he might try it on. I was grateful and ticked at the same time. Clearly a lot of emotional stuff in me still needed to be worked out, but I was so thankful that high dose chemo was not an option at that time. And how great that when it seemed like there was no more treatment available, one was on the horizon all the time! God's timing is perfect. Treatments went smoothly and remissions lasted for twelve to fourteen months for about ten years.

# CHAPTER 16

began to spend more time with my mom, taking her out to lunch at least once a week. One day while we were eating, I asked her to tell me her life story. "I know bits and pieces, Mom, but I'd like to hear it from you." She rose to the occasion.

"When I was born, my mother was sick, and I was sent to live with my Grandmother Lawson. I lived there for eighteen months and then went home to my parents, my older sister and two older brothers. Over the next nine or so years I lived with my mother, father, and siblings but then my dad died suddenly when I was eleven. I got sent back to Grandma Lawson, and her words to me were, 'just like a bad penny you keep showing up,'" Mom said, looking somewhat sad, but more angry. She had been her dad's favorite and now felt alone and abandoned, which became the theme for her life.

Mom was a very gifted artist and during her senior year in high school won the 1939 World's Fair contest in New York City, which was a full scholarship to college to teach art. My grandmother wouldn't let her go as she couldn't afford the room and board. Mom's art teacher offered to pay the room and board with the idea that when she graduated and had a job, she would pay him back. The pride on mom's face as she told this story was unmistakable. "But," she said, "my mother wouldn't let me accept it because she needed me to work in the beauty shop and she told me the art teacher was only making a play for me and really didn't mean it. I knew he did and felt defeated."

A few months afterwards she met my dad, and they married within the year. She went on to say, "We were happy for the first few years, but things began to unravel, and I never felt like I could do anything right in your father's eyes. I tried, and every time I got pregnant, he blamed me." She went into much detail about dad leaving her with five kids, no money, and the electricity about to be turned off necessitating some tough decisions about what to do next. That was when she placed all five of us in foster care. When they got back together, things hadn't improved much.

"No wonder you took drugs and drank, Mom."

"What did you say?" she asked looking somewhat confused.

"I said, no wonder you drank. What were you supposed to do with all that pain and feeling rejected and/or unwanted? There wasn't that much help available for dealing with emotional pain then."

Gradually over the next three years things changed. Little by little, I began to understand that she came to parenthood damaged herself and had no idea how to do anything but care for herself, and when the pain got unbearable, she deadened it with drugs and alcohol. All her hopes and dreams of marriage had been shattered when my father left her, and though they reunited, they never really reconciled. I began to share who I am with her, and she responded lovingly. As the Lord unfolded His plan for our relationship, it grew, and although I remember the events of my life and the feelings of rejection, my mother's simple "I love you" healed many hurts.

Eighty-two years young, still living in the adult home and happy, mom no longer tried to manipulate me and genuinely became interested in my children and grandchildren. The day before Mother's Day, my daughter invited my mother and me to a mother-daughter brunch at her church. During the one-and-one-half hour drive to my daughter Kelly's, mom and I talked about how grateful we are for the healing in our relationship. I told her that if she died tomorrow I had no regrets and with tears threatening to fall from her eyes, she said she felt the same way.

Mom, Kelly, her daughters Katie and Emily, and me

The speaker at the tea that day related the broken relationship she had with her mother and how the walls between them gradually came down before her mom died. My mother was very touched by the talk and reached over and held my hand. I had never felt so much love from or for my mom as I did that moment, and I silently thanked God for answering my prayer of forgiveness twenty-plus years earlier.

On the way back home that evening, mom was quiet at first and then said, "I've started praying at night before I go to sleep and rather than just saying the prayers I learned when I was little, I've been thinking about what I've been praying. There's a line in the Hail Mary that says 'Blessed is the fruit if thy womb, Jesus.' Does that mean that Jesus came out of Mary's womb?"

It suddenly occurred to me that she had never learned the basics of the faith, no matter how many times she had heard the salvation message and hadn't responded. Slowly telling her the Good News of Jesus Christ and his desire for her to be forgiven and spend eternity with Him, her heart opened, and she accepted Jesus as her Savior and Lord in the quiet dark of my car.

What a memorable Mother's Day! I praise God for his faithfulness to me and especially to my mom. His word tells us in 2 Peter 3:9 that "He isn't willing that any should perish, but that all should have everlasting life." Forgiveness only comes easy for Him, not usually for us. Yet He is faithful and will gently lead and guide us into forgiveness no matter how grave the offense. Our relationship grew even more as the Holy Spirit began His incredible work in my mother. We learned to laugh together, whine together, share each other's burdens, and pray for one another.

Meanwhile, Dan and I still had hills and valleys in our life. Dan began having some heart issues and eventually wound up with seven stents in his coronary arteries. After that things went fairly smoothly for a couple of years. We spent a few winters in Florida and were planning another when we went to a routine follow-up appointment with Dan's internist. "What did you guys do about Dan's elevated PSA?" he asked.

"What elevated PSA?" we both said simultaneously.

"Five months ago when you were in, the PSA was 7.4 (normal is under 4)."

"What? And why didn't you call us?"

"I called your urologist," he said like I'd asked a stupid question.

"Yeah and he's probably been waiting for us to call and make an appointment." I was so angry I couldn't talk. I don't like to do dirty anger so decided to wait until I'd cooled down to address the issue of not being notified. We left the office unhappily and called our urologist for an appointment. He saw Dan almost immediately and decided to repeat the PSA and do a more definitive test as well. We learned that doing a PSA in a different laboratory can muddy the picture of what's really going on. The repeat PSA came back at 4.5, so the urologist decided to wait "a few months" to repeat it. The more definitive test showed that he had a great chance of it being malignant, but the decision was to wait. I learned that normal doubling time for PSA is ten years. The next PSA was 14.8, which then necessitated an immediate biopsy. By that time I had addressed the issue of no notification with the internist and explained to him that two phone calls would have been better than none and would he please adjust his office protocols so that patients were notified immediately. He sheepishly agreed.

The biopsy results were not good. Dan's Gleason score from the biopsy was 9. Low numbers (2–7) usually mean the cancer is slow growing and high numbers (8–10) indicated an aggressive form of prostate cancer. We met with a radiation oncologist who informed us that he couldn't give Dan enough radiation to eradicate the tumor without severely damaging his bowel and bladder. He suggested we go to Pittsburgh for cryosurgery, which we did in October of 2002. The tumor was already outside his prostate, which meant it would be raising its ugly head in four to five years. Dan recovered well and we decided to do a few things we'd been putting off.

# CHAPTER 17

"Where should we go first? I asked, "Hawaii or Alaska"? "Let's check prices on both first," he wisely replied.

Our neighbors worked part time at a travel bureau and had just returned from a cruise to Hawaii that they raved about. We asked them to check prices and get back to us. One evening we invited four of our couple friends to our home to speak with our neighbor about the cruise. The more they talked, the more excited we became. The prices were amazingly low and doable for all of us. Three of the four couples signed up with a down payment that night. The other couple had reservations and bowed out. The trip was to be in January of 2003, which was only a few months away, and all we really needed to get was a passport. We pored over the brochures and fantasized about what we'd do and what we'd see.

One couple flew to New Jersey, and the other two drove to the airport. We had to be there at 4 AM. Kathy was the only one who had no problem with that hour as she is an early bird anyway. The rest of us—well that's a different story. We only had to change planes once in Dallas. The next morning as we awoke in the hotel on Waikiki Beach in Oahu, we heard about the Challenger explosion near Houston that had happened the day before. We were heartbroken for the astronauts and their families. We had two days in Oahu before we boarded the ship for the other islands, so we went to the Pearl Harbor Memorial. What a sobering experience that was. Reading all the names of the men killed, some of whom were brothers or fathers and sons, was heart wrenching. Although there were anywhere from 150 to 200 hundred people there at the same time, you could have heard a pin drop. It made all of us appreciate all our armed forces have done and are doing for the people of America.

The next day we boarded the ship to sail to the various Hawaiian Islands. Kathy, Paul and I spent a lot of time in the hot tub on deck. Dan still had some post-surgical issues, so he opted out but stood close by joking and laughing with us. Kathy, Paul, Dan, and I have been good friends for over thirty years. The other couple was Mary and Rick. It was their baby that I delivered on the front seat of the car. They often went off by themselves.

The first day on board the three women went to make plans for excursions. Mountain bike riding (even downhill only) was out of the question because of somebody's knees. We dismissed a number of the options due to our age or lack of zeal. One that did appeal was called "Tubing in the Ditch." We had no idea what it was, but it sounded like fun, so we signed up for that and for a snorkeling trip. The guys just rolled their eyes. Our tubing group consisted of four professional women from Chicago, three of whom were sisters and the fourth a sister-in-law plus a newlywed couple and the six of us.

The trip to our destination was interesting in that we got into more and more remote areas of the island until we were past any evidence of civilization. Kathy is very frightened of critters regardless of size, so we maximized the time by talking about "lions and tigers and bears, oh my." We asked our guides what types of wildlife inhabited the island and were told wild boar and snakes, to which Kathy screamed "Snakes!" She didn't calm down much when she was told they never got more than six to eight inches long.

Our guides stopped along a culvert, and the driver walked down the embankment without further explanation. He returned with a bunch of ti (tee) leaves, which are rather large and considered good luck by the natives. We continued on our trek and ended at a very barren-looking area with four logs lying on the ground and not much else to see. As we left the van, we were each given a miner's helmet complete with lamp and a pair of Japanese fishing socks. The socks were pea-soup green with the big toe separated from the rest of the toes and came to about mid-calf. We all looked lovely as we donned our outfits: ten overweight middle aged adults and two young people outfitted for the time of their lives. The honeymooners were very reticent to join in the hilarity the rest of us older folks were expressing and hung back away from us.

We were then led to a rickety wooden staircase that descended into a canal about ten feet across and given a huge blue inner tube that was to be our mode of transportation through the ditch.

We had no idea.

No one was impressed at that point, and as we boarded our vehicles, we noticed a rather rapid current. Our guides then explained that the ditch had been dug many years ago to bring water from the mountains into the lowlands to water the crops. Our trip was to take about forty-five minutes and was about five miles long. One guide in front and one guide behind the group, we started off spinning round and round with the current, bumping into one another and laughing from the outset. There was no navigating; one went where the current demanded. High banks sported long grasses reaching out into the ditch, and Kathy got caught in a little divot in the bank and started screaming loud and long. She was stuck, and the grasses were freaking her out. Paul was behind me and said, "I never have to wonder where she is" and laughed. Dan rescued her as he was closest, and we were on our way again.

About halfway we entered a very dark tunnel about a mile long. Our guides stopped the group and had us turn on the head-lamps on the helmet, explaining that if we wanted to know what it had been like for the people who dug this ditch, to turn off the lamps and continue along. Some did and some didn't. Kathy screamed every time any part of her touched the walls, which only made the rest of us laugh more. By this time the honey-mooners had joined in the fun. At the end we half expected a feast of some sort. Papaya juice and fresh fruit was our fare. Dan had gone into a porta-potty to change into something dry and came out without a shirt. "Where's your shirt?" I asked. He never went without a shirt even at home.

"Don't need it right now," was all he said.

A few minutes later our male guide took Dan, Rick, and the groom off into a wooded area. The rest of us just looked at each other wondering what the heck was going on. About fifteen minutes later the guys came back all covered with mud on their faces, arms, and chests, each sporting some kind of necklace or headband of woven ti leaves. Our guide introduced Dan as "Chief PuaPua," the head of the tribe, with Rick as second in command and our groom as a trainee.

Our chief!

He explained the hierarchy of clan leadership on the island many years ago. Dan got into his role quite readily, enjoying every moment. The rest of us were hysterical. The banter followed us the entire trip back to the ship.

Upon boarding the ship, Dan stepped up to the two men, checking IDs, and said in a rather boisterous, booming voice, "Chief PuaPua requesting permission for our party to come aboard Sir." Everyone including the checkers was laughing loudly. When we boarded the elevator to go to our rooms, another couple looked quite frightened and huddled in the corner. The rumor on the ship that night was that we had returned from our island trip drunk. We were: on fun and a very good time, but not as they surmised. That was the best time any of us had ever had.

On the island of Maui Rick and Mary went their way and Paul, Kathy, Dan and I decided we would get into the tourist mode. The guys bought Hawaiian shirts to match our baggy island dresses. Kathy and I bought big sun hats. We sure looked the part. We shopped and eventually made our way into a Thomas Kincade gallery. None of us had ever been in an art gallery, so when a man approached us and asked if we wanted to view anything special, we started to say "no," but I noticed Dan standing in front of a lighthouse painting completely mesmerized. The man took us into a room so we could feel what the painter was conveying. Dan began to weep. "Are you okay?" I asked. He couldn't speak. Later he told me that he had seen God's grace in the sun rays through storm clouds.

The four of us went on to have lunch, and when Kathy had to use the restroom, I went with her. "I'm going to go back and buy that painting for Dan. Could you get Paul to distract him, and I'll say I want to go back to another shop to get Danny a tee shirt." She agreed, and Paul suggested he and Dan sit on a bench overlooking the ocean while we went on our errand. The painting was shipped to Mike's house because I wanted to give it to Dan as a birthday gift in April. I thought I could hang it on the wall opposite his favorite chair, and when he became sad about what was going on with him, he could look at the painting, remember our trip, and the grace of God through whatever storms were threatening.

Mike and an electrician friend of his rewired a plug in our living room and installed track lighting on Dan's birthday while we were out to lunch and a movie. Mike was still there when we came home, and I told Dan he could have his birthday present; he just had to find it. We did the "you're getting hot, or you're getting cold" as he looked behind chairs and under beds. Finally he gave up and sat down in his chair. "Look up Dan," I said.

"Where?" he asked.

"Just look up." He finally spotted the painting and began to weep with tears of joy.

"You bought the painting!"

"I did, Happy Birthday my love." He later told me how much that painting meant to him and how even more precious it was because I had bought it for him. He even had a remote so he could adjust the lighting to his taste.

# CHAPTER 18

On Easter Sunday of 2003 mom joined our family for church and dinner. It was probably one of the best times I'd had with her. We spent a lot of time together talking and reminiscing. The next day she wasn't feeling well; by Tuesday she had a fever of 102 degrees and was admitted to the hospital. When I got there she said, "When they asked me what my religion was, I said 'reborn Christian.' Is that right?"

"Sounds a little like refried beans, but it's absolutely right, Mom," I replied and we both laughed. Within two days she was in a coma. Her last words to me were "I love you." The following Monday she suddenly opened her eyes and stared at the far corner of her room with joy radiating from her eyes. "What are you seeing Mom? Tell me please." With that she closed her eyes and took her last breath. She was home at last.

That same spring, while doing my devotions one morning, I heard in my spirit that I was to raise up a leader from within each of the four Bible studies I was leading then to take over in the fall. Thinking it was to write, I was obedient. I now know the purpose of that particular instruction was due to what happened next. Because Dan had already had one heart attack and three angioplasties, any chest pain alerted us. Dan had another heart catheterization, and all his arteries were clear. Our cardiologist was perplexed about the cause of the pain. "We've always wondered if there isn't a gastro-esophageal problem going on at the same time so I'd like to order an endoscopy just to take a look." It seemed reasonable, so we scheduled it. Because I knew the gastroenterologist who was going to perform the procedure, I asked if I could be with Dan, and he agreed. Dan was loopy from the sedation that kept him conscious, so he wasn't following much of the conversation. The doctor motioned me out of the room and told me in the hall that Dan had esophageal cancer.

"How do you know? You just took the biopsy," I said alarmed.

"I can tell by looking at the lesion in his esophagus, but I think we've caught it early. I want you to see a thoracic surgeon as soon as possible." I walked out of the office numb. It had only been ten months since the prostate cancer diagnosis. We were like zombies through the weekend but decided God knew what was going on and would give us what we needed to cope with whatever happened. Dan spent a lot of time meditating on the painting, and I was glad once again that I had bought it for him.

The thoracic surgeon was not as optimistic. "This could just be the tip of the iceberg," he announced. "We'll have to do more extensive testing to be sure." The final results showed that the cancer was wrapped around Dan's esophagus and the doctor recommended immediate surgery . "We will have two surgeons in the OR at the same time, a gastric surgeon to do the biopsy of the lymph nodes, and if the nodes are negative, he will remove the upper third of Dan's stomach; I will then remove all but four inches of his esophagus. If the nodes are positive, we will place a feeding tube and close him up so we can do radiation and chemo first." It took a few days for the surgeon's schedules to be coordinated. In the meantime, Dan wanted to go to Maurer's Funeral Home and make arrangements "just in case I don't make it."

"Why don't we make both our arrangements at the same time? Then the kids won't have to do that when the time comes for either one of us." It was a very sobering experience. We were both pretty quiet on the way home but knew it was the right thing to do. When Dan had the pre-admission blood work done, it showed that his blood wasn't clotting fast enough for the surgery. The Coumadin he was on had already been discontinued, but his numbers still weren't safe for surgery, which had been scheduled two days hence. "No problem" the surgeon said, "it'll be within a normal range by the time we do the surgery. I'll just repeat the blood test the morning he is admitted." I wasn't comfortable with that decision at all but didn't say anything.

The night before his surgery I found Dan on a stool putting fiberglass on a spot on one of the motor home compartment doors. "What are you doing out here?" I asked.

"Fixing this door in case something happens to me and you have to sell the rig," he replied matter of factly. He was very frightened and really didn't know how to express it, but in his love for me, he was taking care of things. I had bumped into a good pastor friend of mine (from a different church) at the grocery store that evening, and he asked me how I was doing. Bursting into tears I told him what Dan was facing the next day. He immediately stopped in the flow of customer traffic and prayed with me on the spot. I just knew God was in control.

The morning of surgery, the Coumadin levels were still elevated, but the anesthesiologist decided to go ahead. Again I asked myself if this was a good decision. We were allowed to stay with him, and our pastor came to pray with us. It seemed like we were in the waiting room forever when someone called to tell us that they had just taken Dan into the OR. "What? He's been down there for four hours already and you're just getting started!" I blurted.

"It took some time to get all the lines in we needed before we could begin the surgery. His surgeon will be out to speak with you as soon as the results from the nodes are complete," he explained. A few hours later the gastric surgeon came to the waiting room to tell us he wasn't able to retrieve any nodes, so they decided to proceed with the surgery, and he had done his part.

Later that evening the thoracic surgeon came to tell us Dan was out of surgery, and that ten nodes had been retrieved and sent for results. Dan should be in recovery shortly. A couple of hours later, a nurse from the recovery room came to me and said that Dan had been extubated but that he was in so much pain they were going to put the tube back in and put him in a drug-induced coma for overnight. She asked if I wanted to see him first. All of our kids had gone to get something to eat, so my pastor went with me.

Dan was writhing in pain. "Help me, Gloria!" he cried. I explained why he was getting another tube put in and that he'd be in ICU overnight. Our pastor prayed with both of us.

"I'll be with you until you're comfortable," I promised. About an hour later he was in ICU and comfortable. We all went home for some rest, but I said to his nurse before I left, "Please call me for anything during the night. This is my husband, my soulmate, and the love of my life." She was gracious and promised she would. I slept fitfully and couldn't wait to get back to the hospital early the next morning. Dan's condition worsened progressively. For the next ten days everyone wondered hour by hour if he'd make it. He had every complication imaginable. Beginning with aspiration pneumonia he progressed to metabolic and respiratory acidosis, a mild stroke, congestive heart failure, pancreatic failure, kidney failure, and adult respiratory distress syndrome (ARDS) which is similar to what premature babies get called hyaline membrane disease or respiratory distress syndrome.

The anesthesiologists who care for all ventilated patients in this particular hospital were not sure from day to day what the outcome would be. We prayed like we'd never prayed before.

Family and friends were there with us most of the time and brought us encouragement and very often food. The nurses and doctors let me stay with Dan as long as I wanted to, which was usually from ten to twelve hours a day. The only reason I went home at night was to get some rest because without it, the potential was there for me to get sick as well.

The ventilator was set at maximum levels, and it was questionable whether or not he'd be able to breathe on his own without it even though he was taking some breaths on his own. From day two onward, I kept a running log of what was happening medically, who visited, and what each person brought, whether food, a word of encouragement, or comfort. To keep the nurses from getting paranoid about what I was writing down, I reassured them each that if I were the one in the bed and missing day after day, I'd want someone to keep a log so I could get up to speed when I woke up. I assumed Dan would want to know as well.

By day ten, the anesthesiologists began to say they were "cautiously optimistic" that Dan would recover. "Will he have a brain?" I asked. His blood gas levels had been critically low at times, and I was worried about possible brain damage. That same day when I was there alone, which was very unusual, the thoracic surgeon came in to tell me that two of his gastric (not esophageal) nodes were positive, which meant his cancer was Stage 3. Waving his arm over Dan, he said rather tersely, "you may want to rethink what you're doing here and consider what you want to do if his heart stops." He then turned on his heel and left.

I was devastated as I'd just begun to hope. I knew God had everything under control, but I was scared. The doctor had told the nurse to have me sign a DNR. I couldn't. I knew Dan wouldn't want to live if he recovered but wasn't himself, but I needed time to pray about the right thing to do. It took me all weekend amid many tears, and finally by Monday, I signed it with many contingencies. It was the hardest thing I'd ever had to do, and I hoped I had made the right decision. By then, the doctors decided if Dan couldn't be weaned off the ventilator, he'd have to have a tracheotomy. The decision was made to reduce the sedation slowly and turn down the settings on the ventilator gradually to see how he tolerated it. He did fairly well, and the decision was made to stop all sedation and turn off the ventilator at seven o'clock in the morning a few days later.

Entering Dan's room in ICU at 6:30 the next morning, I prayed for God's will. Dan was waking up, knew me and his eyes reflected all the questions he had. "It's sink or swim time," the anesthesiologist said as he prepared to remove the tube. I was asked to step out of the room, which I did reluctantly. A few minutes later I was called back into the room, and Dan was breathing fairly comfortably on his own.

"Praise the Lord." I breathed silently. He had his ups and downs respiratory wise but stabilized after about twelve hours. I think I held my breath the whole time. He was now nineteen days post-op.

Besides the damage to his lungs, our next hurdle was ICU psychosis. Many people with long stays in ICU experience it for various lengths of time. Dan had a prolonged case. The nurses tried a sleep schedule for him. I suggested he be put in an ICU room with a TV to try and orient him. He knew me but that was about all. Having no idea he was in the hospital or why, he acted out and became quite belligerent.

Finally, after five days, it was decided to put him in a regular room on a regular floor where he could have more visitors and a more normal day/night routine. I told him later that for those five days and the next five days he was meaner than a junk yard dog. Even on his worst days during our marriage he had never said some of the things he hurled at me during the psychotic period. I finally asked for a psychiatrist to see him, to which his caregivers agreed. She put him on an antipsychotic drug "just for now and then a week after his mind clears."

The kids had decided that after three-plus weeks of my being there long hours every day I needed a break. A group of women from church and I had bought tickets months prior for Women of Faith in Rochester, New York. My kids wanted me to go and set up a schedule for one of them to be with Dan the whole time I was gone, which was only overnight. The evening before I was supposed to leave, Dan looked at me and said, "Honey, didn't I have surgery or something?" He was back.

I could have done a glory, hallelujah dance and decided right then and there I wasn't going anywhere. It had been six weeks since his surgery. We had a lot to catch up on.

"Yes, you did. Six weeks ago."

"Six weeks! What the heck happened? I don't remember anything!" he exclaimed. "Are you sure it's been six weeks? Didn't I have surgery or something?" The poor guy was perplexed that he had lost a month and a half of his life. I gave him the abbreviated version, not wanting to overload him with too much information right away. He still couldn't get himself out of bed or shower on his own. About all he could do was feed himself and brush his teeth, and that exhausted him.

# CHAPTER 19

B ecause Dan had stabilized but was still very weak, the doctors and the discharge planner told me I should start looking for a rehab center for him. "I can take care of him at home," I stated.

"It'll be too much for you," they replied.

"I don't think so!" I retorted more emphatically than I intended. They all disagreed with me just as strongly. Mike and I looked at rehab centers close to home. Dan was too sick for most and not able to do three hours of physical therapy a day, so he could not be accepted at another. The crowning blow came one morning when I was told that as soon as the doctor wrote the orders for him to go to rehab we had to take any available bed within a fifty-mile radius.

"How is that supposed to be easier on me? I already spend ten to twelve hours or more a day here and now you want to add a one hundred-mile trip per day besides?" I went home that night very angry and cried out my despair to God. "Open doors Lord, or make it possible for me to bring him home. He'll do better in his own bed, his own chair, and with his own dog on his lap and the remote in his hand." I was beginning to decide our best option was for me to bring him home. One evening Dan begged me to take him home.

"I will, Dan, on one condition."

"What's that?" He asked.

"You cannot yell *at* me. You can yell about anything but not *at* me. The minute you start blaming me for what happened, I'm out of here (I never would have left). I know this has been tough on you, but it hasn't been easy for any of us, either. I can't go through the angst of what your ten days of ICU psychosis was. I spent more time in the waiting room crying at your angry outbursts than in the room with you. I understand you will be and are probably frustrated and you can yell about that to get it off your chest but not at me. Okay?"

He agreed. The next day I met once again with the discharge planner and explained to her the frustration of finding a rehab center and informed her I was taking him home. "I'm taking him home with or without your blessing, but he's going home. I'd appreciate your blessing and help because I'll need supplies at home for his tube feeding, oxygen, physical therapy, etc. Besides I'd like a nurse to check on him at least once a week. I'm his wife, and I don't want to be the only one evaluating him because my assessment could be subjective." She looked at me like I had two heads but realized I was serious and made arrangements for the home discharge planner to meet with me. I felt like my guns were loaded, cocked, and ready to fire.

Becky, the home discharge planner, came to visit that same day. She was pleasant and asked me what was going on, listening to my response respectfully. At one point she said, "Your last name is Manns, right?" We both nodded our heads. "My dad was a sheriff in Onondaga County. You're a retired police officer, right Dan?" We both nodded again and she began to talk animatedly with Dan about all the mutual people they knew. God had provided someone who related well to us and did everything she could for Dan to go home.

Two weeks later, after Dan had successfully walked two stairs and back, he was discharged. The effort exhausted him so I hired a wheelchair cab to transport him home. I was not sure I was strong enough to help him out of the car, get his walker, and help him to walk the short distance into the house. Best $40.00 I ever spent. He couldn't keep his eyes open once the transporters had him safely in his chair. Thankfully it was only about ten steps to our bathroom and bedroom, so I was reasonably sure with the right timing, he could make those trips. He was very weak, and his muscles had atrophied a lot. Each morning I'd help him to the bathroom, wash and dress him, and shave his handsome face. About all he had energy for was to brush his teeth.

A day or two later I found him in our living room rocking back and forth in his chair saying repeatedly, "I can't yell at Mom, I can't yell at Mom."

"What's the matter?" I asked.

"I can't yell at you, but I'm so angry about the way I am. I feel like a weak old man and wonder if I should have even had the surgery," he blurted out.

"You can yell about that Dan. Get it off your chest. You'll feel better." He did, and I reassured him he just couldn't blame me but to feel free to vent his frustration anytime he wanted. A couple of days later he wanted to be in the bathroom alone. When he called for me he had shaved himself and was about as proud as he could be. Each day he got stronger and tried doing other things for himself without overdoing.

Six days later Dan was very weak and seemed to be going backwards. I thought he looked very pale, and his breathing was somewhat labored. When the nurse came, she checked his vital signs and agreed; she called the doctor for an order for blood work and told us to go to the emergency room right away. Dan protested but felt lousy enough that he didn't put up much of a fight. It took forever to find out what the problem was, but they finally discovered that his blood was not clotting, so he was bleeding internally. "The results of this bloodwork make *me* bleed!" exclaimed the doctor. "His oral meds are pooling in his stomach, and then he gets them all at once. His Coumadin levels are off the chart. I'm going to give him two units of blood, four units of fresh frozen plasma, and a shot of vitamin K to reverse the effects."

His breathing seemed to be getting worse, and I noticed that his IV fluids were going in at a rapid rate. "You have got to slow down the fluids. He just got out of congestive heart failure and you're going to put him right back in at that rate," I said not too kindly as I was frustrated. They slowed the infusion some and about 3 AM he was transferred to the same room from which he'd been discharged. By then he was feeling better, and most of the staff knew that he was back and came in to say hello. He had to use the bathroom and wanted the nurses and physical therapist to see how he'd improved in just a week so he got himself out of bed, used his walker, and went into the bathroom. Everyone was applauding and singing his praises when I thought I heard him call my name. I opened the door and he was as blue as a grape. It took all of us to get him back to bed and the doctor was called emergently. Scans were ordered, and when the doctor took me aside I knew he wasn't going to say anything good.

"He has a massive clot in his left lung, and it has knocked out all the perfusion (blood flow) in that lung. I don't expect he'll make it through the weekend. I'm sorry but I believe his clotting was overcorrected in the emergency room, and his lungs are already severely compromised," the doctor said solemnly. Dan hadn't heard that prognosis, which was a good thing as he was struggling enough just to breathe.

We prayed and waited all weekend, and by Monday morning he seemed to be breathing easier. The first words out of his mouth were: "When can I eat?" Only God! The doctors couldn't believe their eyes or stethoscopes as they listened to his lungs. No one said "miracle," but I knew I had just witnessed a huge one. He was not allowed to eat because the doctors thought the reason for his admission was a paralyzed stomach. He was fed a radiation-loaded egg salad sandwich the next afternoon and placed under a scanner to see how soon his stomach emptied. Two and a half hours later the sandwich had not moved. From then on Dan could not eat solids but had to rely and live on tube feedings. This for a man who *loved* to eat. He was discharged two weeks later.

# CHAPTER 20

Home again. Dan gradually regained some of his strength and was able to walk without his walker. He still tired very quickly but felt good about his progress. One afternoon he was very quiet sitting in his chair petting our dog, Tigger. "What are you thinking about?" I asked.

"I'm wondering if I could ask you to do something for me."

"Sure. What is it?"

"Would you grow your hair out for me one more time? I love it long."

I had very long hair when we dated and for several years after we were married. But I had cut it short when I started working in labor and delivery because I had to wear scrub caps almost all day long or all night long, depending on the shift, so it had been short for a long time.

"Sure," I said. I felt like that was the least I could do for him after all he'd been through. It wasn't easy especially at the in-between stages, and frequently when I was frustrated Dan would lovingly tell me that he appreciated that I'd tried and to cut it if I wanted. "No Dan, this is as important to me as it is to you. I'll get through this rough patch." And so it grew.

We went on a few camping trips, and although he thoroughly enjoyed the outings, it took a couple of days for him to recover after we returned home. He felt bad because he couldn't do much of the work of loading and unloading the motor home but felt good driving it. We now had to include tube feeding supplies and oxygen as well as emergency supplies, but it soon became routine and no big deal to us.

I began experiencing more shortness of breath and intermittent chest pain that summer, so I went to my cardiologist for a check-up. He ordered a CT of my chest, which showed a spot on my lung. On my next visit to my oncologist, she said the scan showed a possible pneumonia and that she wasn't worried about it but wanted me on antibiotics. I didn't feel sick and sure didn't think I had pneumonia but was so focused on Dan that I really didn't process the information like I usually did.

Six weeks later the doctor wanted a repeat of the CT scan to make sure the pneumonia was gone. I didn't even question it until much later as I was much more concerned about making sure that I could coordinate Dan's scans and mine to save us a trip to the city. At my next visit to the oncologist, I asked what the CT scan report said. As the NP started reading it, her color blanched, and she left the room to get the doctor.

"The spot is still there," she said. "I'd like to get a biopsy as soon as possible."

"What? Are you worried about this?"

"No," she answered, "but with your history, I'd like to get a biopsy anyway."

I wasn't worried either but thought it strange that I had to go through it. Dan still wasn't up to par, and I hated leaving him but wouldn't let him go with me as I knew it would set him back with fatigue. I began to question in my mind why the repeat CT scan as an x-ray isn't usually repeated with pneumonia. Three days later, on a Friday afternoon, my oncologist called me. "I have the biopsy results," she said.

"And everything is okay. Right?"

"Gloria, I'm sorry to have to tell you that you have lung cancer."

"What! You said you weren't worried."

"I wasn't," she replied to my outburst. "I'd like you to see a thoracic surgeon as soon as possible. Do you want to have the same one who operated on Dan?"

"Absolutely not! I cannot put Dan through what I went through with that doctor's cavalier bedside manner. Who do you recommend?" She gave me the name of a surgeon and apologized profusely that she'd had to tell me the news over the telephone. The nurse practitioners who worked with her told me later that they had heard a blood curdling scream come from her office. When they investigated, she was in tears looking at my biopsy results. Dan was also a cancer patient in that office, and she knew what we had dealt with the past twenty months.

Dan wanted to go camping that weekend, which we did. He usually stayed in bed until noon waiting for his tube feeding to finish. I had taken our two dogs for a walk and was doing my quiet time at the campground. I usually read two or three devotionals plus the Bible. In *Our Daily Bread* there is a recommended scripture reading, but for me, it's not usually enough, so I frequently will read the whole chapter or two. This particular day the reading was from I Peter 5. It stopped at verse 7, which says "cast all your anxieties on Him because He cares for you." I read further, and verses 10–11 seemed to jump off the page into my heart. "And the God of all Grace who calls you to eternal life in Christ Jesus, after you have suffered for a little while, will Himself make you strong, firm, and steadfast. To Him be the glory forever and ever. Amen."

I grabbed onto that scripture and committed it to memory. It got me through some tough times during the surgery, post-operative period, and complications requiring rehospitalization. About a month after my surgery Dan wanted to go camping again. "If you want to go, we'll go, but I need help packing and unpacking the camper. It still hurts too much to lift."

"No problem," he said. I knew he still wasn't up to par, but between the both of us we managed at a much slower pace. Each day for the preceding month I woke up in the morning relatively free of severe pain. About a half an hour later each day it felt like someone shoved a machete into the back of my ribcage and twisted it until I had enough pain meds in me to make it tolerable by mid-afternoon.

The night before we left to go camping, I told God that my definition of a "little while" was up. Could He please make the machete-like pain stop? The next morning I got up as usual without severe pain and was busy doing the last minute packing when I realized I'd been up for an hour and that pain wasn't there. I never had it again. Ten months later I had a lump in my breast and began to think we couldn't keep doing this every-ten-month catastrophe stuff. Thankfully it was benign, and that was the end of the cycle.

Dan was never back to the state of health he had been prior to his surgeries, but he did amazingly well. Although he tired more readily, he was like the energizer bunny and kept on keeping on. We did take two more winter hiatuses from the cold and went to Florida for a couple of months. The last year we went, I had to drive both ways as Dan's depth perception and balance were being affected by metastasis of the esophageal cancer to his brain. He'd think he was walking in a straight line and walk right into a wall. He had quit driving the previous summer as he kept going off the road. "It would be just fine with me if we both died at the same time, Dan, but I don't think either one of us could live with hurting someone else," I said after a rather scary drive with him.

By the fall of 2006 we knew we had to sell the motor home as Dan was becoming weaker and weaker. We took a huge hit on the sale of the rig but cannot put a price on the enjoyment we had for the years we travelled in it. By then the prostate cancer had raised its ugly head as well.

Our family was pretty sure that unless the Lord intervened, we would be having our last Christmas with Dan that year. He kept saying he wanted a Red Ryder BB gun for Christmas. We all kept telling him "he'd shoot his eye out." He wanted to go shopping for me, so Mike and MaryKay packed his walker, wheelchair, and him into their vehicle and off they went. He was very tired when he got back but had a grin on his face from ear to ear. That was the first Christmas present he'd ever bought for me that he'd been able to keep a secret until Christmas. He had bought three beautiful outfits for me. Our whole family spent Christmas Day at our son Mike and MaryKay's home. Mike had bought Dan the BB gun for his Christmas present, and the look on Dan's face when he opened it was priceless. He was like a young boy again. Thankfully we have many photographs of that momentous day.

Like a little boy again

# CHAPTER 21

D an's pain was increasing, and his comfort level was short-lived at best. He began sleeping a lot. One night, however, we had gone through the bedtime routine, and he was settled in with his oxygen and tube feeding running. I was just coming through the bedroom door when he asked me, "Would you think I was stupid if I asked you if I could brush your hair?"

"No, not at all," I literally choked out the words.

"Then please get your brush." As I sat on the edge of the bed with him brushing my very long hair, he'd stroke it with one hand and brush it with the other as he said, "Your hair is so beautiful. Thank you for growing it out for me." He couldn't see the tears streaming down my cheeks. I don't know that I had ever felt such intimacy before. We hadn't been able to have sex since his prostate surgery, which really bothered him. He even asked me one time if I was going to leave him because we couldn't do "it."

In April of 2007 we celebrated Dan's seventieth birthday.

Our children and spouses with our grandchild Susanna

He was pale, weak, and tired but put on a good front for our children and grandchildren. He told Pat that day that he wanted to go to his place in the country and shoot his Red Ryder BB gun. A few weeks later as we stood on Pat and Holly's front porch with our son Pat, his son Jonah, and Dan all raising rifles to their shoulders to shoot at empty cans, I was astounded at Dan's resolve to make a memory with his son and grandson. This was a time that would be remembered for a very long while.

Our grandson Jonah

The following month it was time for hospice care. I must admit I was afraid it was a death sentence for Dan and that his care would be minimal at best. I couldn't have been more wrong. I have never met more caring, concerned, and giving people than those who are employed by hospice. Each one seemed to genuinely care not only for Dan but for the rest of the family as well and offered helpful suggestions to make it easier on all of us.

Pain management was one of the biggest issues we faced. He would sometimes sit and cry as he was in so much pain. Dan was not normally a person who cried. Hospice doctors do not usually make house calls to patients, but Dan had two visits to get his pain under control. Once it was controlled, his sense of humor returned rather abruptly. For example, one evening I was sewing an heirloom christening gown for Hilary and Greg's new baby girl when I stepped into the doorway of the living room and asked our son Danny if he was going to be there for a few minutes as I needed to run to the store to get buttons so I could make buttonholes.

"You're going out again!" Dan shouted at me. "What's the matter? Am I getting to be too much for you that you want to get away from me? You were gone *all day* yesterday and now you want to go out again?" he continued. I had gone to a bridal shower the day before for a dear family friend with Dan's encouragement because I hadn't been out of the house in over two weeks. Danny had stayed with his dad; I was gone about four hours, and all had gone well.

"Dan, I don't have to get the buttons now," I sobbed. "What is the matter that you're so upset?"

He smiled, shook his upper body slightly, folded his arms across his chest, and said very pompously, "There now I feel better. I've exercised my masculinity."

"You were just fooling around?" I said, still crying.

"Yup." I settled down and we hugged and laughed together. I still don't know why I reacted the way I did as this was a common occurrence between us but always when I least expected it. I didn't realize then just how vulnerable I felt. Oh, and I did go get the buttons.

One of the things Dan wanted to do before he couldn't was to go to Sight and Sound Theatre in Lancaster, Pennsylvania to see *In the Beginning*. Danny, Pat, Holly, and their children went with us, and we had a wonderful time together. In the show, Adam had just died and Eve was in front of the curtain while scene changes were going on. She was clinging to a rock, crying and singing "Adam, Adam what am I going to do without you?" Dan put his arms around me and we both sobbed. After forty-six years of marriage, we realized we weren't going to be together much longer, and it hurt.

Dan insisted the hospital bed be in our bedroom right next to mine so we could cuddle. The problem was the side rail wasn't very comfortable on my back or side, so I bought a foam noodle that kids use in the pool, sliced it partway down the middle, and slid it over the bar. Our nighttime routine was just that "routine," until we finally got settled into bed. We would read Oswald Chambers and if we understood it, discuss it. Then he'd pray, I'd pray, and we'd talk about anything and everything. Dan had always been afraid of our being separated for any reason but especially something as permanent as death. Many nighttime discussions centered on questions such as: What happens when we die? Will we be married in heaven? Why can't we both die at the same time?

Psalm 139 helped us in so many ways and we read that and Psalm 23 every night. In Psalm 139 God tells us that (1) He knew each and every one of us before the foundation of the earth, (2) He knit us together in our mother's womb, (3) we have been fearfully and wonderfully made, and (4) all the days for me or you were written in His book before there was one. That Psalm, as God's Word does, comforted us during a difficult time. We talked about funeral arrangements, what he wanted to be laid out in, and if there was there anything else he needed or wanted before the Lord took him home.

One particular evening Dan asked me if I thought we'd make it to our fiftieth wedding anniversary.

"Do you want an honest answer Honey?"

"Yes, I do."

"No, I don't think we will but we've known each other for fifty years," I said, hoping that would help.

"I so wanted you to have your twenty-five years," he said woefully. I chuckled as that statement stemmed from an argument we'd had on our twenty-fifth anniversary. Dan was in the van in the driveway, and I was standing outside when he said something that set me off. I had learned early in our marriage not to argue with him because it only gave him more ammo for the next disagreement. So I'd remain silent while he ranted, and that only made him madder. On this particular day, I lost it and let him have it verbally both barrels. He started laughing.

"What's so funny?" I shouted at him.

"I wondered how long you'd take my guff before you'd finally had enough," he said with a smirk on his face.

"This has been a test?" I screamed at him. He didn't say anything so I kept on. "Okay, bucko, you've had the first twenty-five years; the next twenty-five are mine! Things will be different. There will be no more screaming matches; we will wait until we've quieted down before we discuss calmly whatever the issue is. We will not outtalk each other; you will be quiet when I'm talking, and I will be quiet when you're talking. We will agree to disagree without it being disloyalty. Got it? And if we make it to fifty you can have the next twenty-five if either of us remembers."

All he said was "Okay." It took a long time for us to perfect the new approach, but things were so much better between us. We had both come to the marriage with a ton of baggage, and this was another way of shedding the unnecessary stuff. From then on, on each anniversary one of us would say, "Does it get any better than this?" And the next year we'd ask the same question and be amazed that it was indeed better. So Dan wanted me to have my entire twenty-five years.

"I've had more than enough, Honey, and don't feel slighted in the least." I said. "When you hear Jesus call your name, you go. I'll be okay. I won't like it, but I'll be okay, and I'll be with you one day forever in God's Kingdom."

One of our last pictures together

Dan began having even more trouble walking and making it to the bathroom or the living room to watch TV. We moved the hospital bed into the living room so he'd be close to his chair and able to watch TV from bed if he wanted to. I slept on the couch to be near him. It seemed as though the cancer had come back with a vengeance as he deteriorated right before our eyes over the next week. He never did get out of bed to sit in his chair and often didn't make it to the bathroom. By this time he was going downhill neurologically as well. He knew each of us and could communicate but often didn't make sense. He was unaware of his incontinence at this point.

# CHAPTER 22

M y sister Jan came to see Dan for a couple of days and had planned on going back home but stayed for ten. I don't know what I would have done without her. She did laundry as we often had to change Dan's sheets; cooked; kept track of all the food being brought in by friends, family and church family; who came to visit; and so on. That allowed me to spend all of my time with Dan. I often got into bed with him just to cuddle. He loved it, and we savored every moment.

Our kids stayed for most of the last ten days of Dan's life and spent quality time with him when he was awake and alert. My brother Ben spent some time with him as well and wanted Dan to know how much he appreciated the fact that Dan had been a surrogate dad to him. We were all especially blessed by that time as sad as it was. We all knew we were saying goodbye in our own way.

Two mornings prior to Dan's passing, he had vomited a large amount and aspirated into his lungs. He had difficulty breathing for about twenty minutes, and we thought that might be the end. He recovered, but I knew his body couldn't handle the assault. He'd had aspiration pneumonia eleven times in the previous year, which had taken a lot out of him each time. He began to run a high fever and become less responsive.

That night we decided as a family to give him a bath as he was very sweaty and had been incontinent. My sons and son-in-law all helped with lifting, MaryKay ran for anything I needed, and Kelly handed me one wet washcloth after another. When we'd finished and changed his bed I noticed my sister standing in the doorway weeping. "Are you okay"? I asked.

"Have you ever done that as a family before?"

"No. Why?"

"That was the most beautiful, sacred thing I've ever seen. I could see and feel the love that each of you have for him." she said. "You all maintained his dignity and were so loving in the way you touched him," she continued.

That was the last day Dan responded to any of us. We all knew the time was drawing short. The next morning he was totally unresponsive and had a fever of over 105. We bathed him again that night just to cool him off, fairly certain that he would be with Jesus before morning. We stood around his bed and prayed as a family that Jesus would come for him soon. Danny had to go to work that night, and I mentioned to him that he might want to say goodbye to his dad before he left.

"I've been saying goodbye for the last three nights, Mom. Please call me if he goes during the night." I promised I would. Pat had to take his wife home as their three kids had been with a sitter all day, and it was getting late, so they left. Mike, my restless one, goes for a drive when he's stressed, so he took off in his truck for a while. Kelly, Mike's wife MaryKay, my sister Jan, and I began our vigil. Dan had told me he wanted to die in my arms at home, and I had promised that as much as that was in my power, he would. The four of us sat around his bed from about 11PM on. I held him in my arms, and we all talked to him and one another softly. The evening was warm with a gentle breeze, so our windows were opened, and we had the lights turned down but on. I had taken off the blood pressure cuff, oxygen, and oximetry as everything was redundant at that point. He hated the oxygen and at that point it wasn't benefitting him at all.

About 2:15AM, Kelly asked me if I had chimes on my porch.

"No Honey, I don't. Why?"

"I hear chimes. Do you, Aunt Jan, or MaryKay?" They each said they didn't.

"Mom, do your neighbors have chimes, because I hear chimes, and they're getting closer," she said.

"I've never heard chimes in this room in all the years we've lived here."

"Mom, they're getting closer. Are you sure you can't hear them?"

"Honey, I wish I could hear what you're hearing, but I don't. I'm sorry." With that Kelly shuddered from head to toe.

"Honey, are you okay?" I was concerned for her as up until a few days before, she had been sure her dad would recover.

"Didn't anyone feel that gust of wind that went through here?" she asked. We all said we hadn't but reassured her that we believed her.

"That's funny. I didn't feel it on my skin either," she whispered.

"Oh, Mom, the chimes are going away." By this time we were all weeping softly. Over the course of the next five minutes or so, Kelly kept mentioning that the chimes were going away. Finally she said; "Oh, Mom, the chimes are gone." With that Dan took in one breath and let it out and was gone. Fifteen-plus years of pain were no longer evident on his face, and he was as peaceful as I'd ever seen him.

My sister told me later that unbeknownst to me she had put the oximeter back on Dan's finger while we were sitting around the bed.

"When Kelly was saying that she could hear the chimes, all his numbers stayed the same, but as soon as she started saying the chimes were going away, all his numbers started dropping, and when she said they were gone, there were only zeroes," she explained. We all stood up, clapped our hands, and praised the Lord. Dan was now safe in His Arms. I called our sons; Mike and Pat came back to the house, and Danny was home by morning. Our pastor came when I called him in the middle of the night to comfort and encourage us.

The next few days were a blur at best. We knew Dan didn't have much longer but were surprised at the numbness we each felt afterwards. I was on my way out the door with my sister and daughter to get thank-you cards for the people performing various parts of Dan's memorial service when I ran back into the house, explaining that I had to let Dan know where I was going. I returned to the car saddened.

Police officers from four different agencies attended the calling hours. There was an honor guard outside the funeral home doors and one on either side of Dan's casket. With precision and respect, they changed guard every hour. I asked my boys if they had arranged for the guard, and they had not. "It's what we do for a fallen comrade, Mom," Mike told me later. Between 800 and 1000 of our friends and family came that evening to pay their respects.

The morning of the funeral, all four agencies went to the funeral home to escort the hearse to the church. Inside the church, on three sides, police officers stood at attention for the entire service. Four police officers on motorcycles went before the procession to the cemetery, stopping traffic at each light. One police car escorted the procession, and two more followed at the rear of the two-plus mile line of cars. As we drove by the police department from which Dan had retired, everyone was outside saluting Dan as the procession passed by. We went by a small park where one little four or five year old boy was playing by himself. When he saw the hearse he saluted. Brought tears to my eyes. As we drove through the city of Syracuse a homeless man took off his hat and laid it over his heart. In my heart, I was blessed by both occurrences. A man of integrity and importance to his family, and to God had passed away, honored by two unlikely people who didn't even know him.

From then on, especially after everyone had gone home after the service, I didn't really feel safe in my home of forty-three years. I began having nightmares of people trying to break in. I hated going out and walking back in later to a dark, empty house. Although I hadn't slept through the night for over four years and no more than two hours at a time for the ten days before Dan died, I had trouble sleeping. Bedtime and night was tortuous. I felt like a little girl again sleeping in a big house, alone and afraid. Reminding myself that I am never alone helped, but I missed having Dan beside me.

A few weeks later, one of the members of the retreat team that I had worked with for years invited a group of us to her home on the lake for lunch. As we reminisced about our ministries together over the years, I realized that God had given us a bond of friendship that transcended age, marital status, or any other demographic. The group asked me to share with them the story of Dan's home going, which I did but not without tears.

About a week later I received a note from one of the gals at the luncheon. She had attended one of the first Bible studies I led and wasn't about to believe at that time that Christ had forgiven her. She had so many questions then and at times seemed even hostile but eventually bowed her knee to the One and Only Christ. Her note essentially said that she had been blessed by Dan's story. She mentioned that in the Old Testament when the high priest went into the Holy of Holies, he had little bells around the bottom of his robe so those outside would know that he was alive. "I've been reading in Hebrews," she wrote, "that Jesus is our High Priest, and I'm wondering that if the chimes Kelly heard might not have been Jesus Himself coming to escort Dan home." Twenty years prior she had given me a rough time about faith in Christ and now was encouraging me with God's Word. I never cease to be amazed at how God meets us where we are and comforts us when we least expect it.

0/20/2007

From left to right: My brother Don, me, my sister Jan, and my brother Ben at a wedding

My birthday that year was hard for me. I didn't want to stay home and get up on my birthday missing the red roses and card that Dan had placed on our dining room table. So I decided to go to my daughter Kelly's in Rochester for the weekend. Mike had asked me to let him know when I was on my way home on Sunday night. It was late as I dreaded walking into an empty house, but I called Mike anyway. He asked me to stop by his house. "But Mike, it's late, and you both have to work in the morning."

"That's okay, Mom. We want to show you something." We had begun moving some of my stuff to their house, and they had painted two rooms for me for whenever I decided to move. Thinking that was the reason for stopping, I did. When I'd been there for about an hour, I got ready to leave, and Mike and MaryKay put on their jackets too.

"Where are you two going?" I asked.

"We're going with you to load up a few more boxes," Mike answered.

"But Mike it's late. It can wait until another day. There's no hurry."

"No, Mom. We're coming with you." Arriving at my house four miles away we all walked in together. The surprise of my life was waiting for me on the dining room table. A rose and baby's breath flower arrangement awaited me. Attached was a note from all of my children which read:

Dear Mom,

The pink roses represent your children and their spouses who love you.

The baby's breath represents the multitudes of family, friends, and church family who love you.

The red rose is from dad, your soul mate, who loves you.

The white rose represents God who defines love and purity and whose love covers us all.

The white and red rose are together now, but someday we will all be together.

All of us wish you a Happy Birthday and love YOU very much!

Needless to say, I cried with tears of joy that my children were so thoughtful. When the flowers eventually died, Mike and I bought silk ones, arranging them exactly as the others. I laminated the note, and they both sit on my bedside table to remind me how much God loves me through my children.

# CHAPTER 23

As time went by I realized that my house didn't feel like a home without Dan. When we bought it forty-two years earlier, it was the first time in my life I felt secure, but without Dan, it just wasn't the same. My daughter in law MaryKay suggested I move in with them through the holidays to make it easier on me, which I did.

Just before Christmas I had a much needed joint replacement in my right hand, so I was going to need help for a while anyway, and it seemed to be the wisest choice. I stayed through the holidays and for the seven weeks my arm was in a cast. We all decided then that the best thing to do was clean out my house and get it ready to sell. Pat and Holly announced they were expecting another baby due in May, exactly nine months after Dan died. I mentioned to Kelly that I thought it was neat that as Dan was going to heaven, the baby was on his/her way here. "Nope, Mom. Dad got there first and picked one out."

"Oh my, we're really in trouble now," I said smiling. Holly later told me that the last thing she said to Dan was they were planning on having another baby and if it was a boy, his middle name would be Daniel. There are too many Daniels in both families for another one to have that as a first name. Alyssa Rose was born May 15 and is a delight. A neighbor of Pat and Holly mentioned the day she arrived home that Alyssa looked just like her grandpa. I didn't see it, but she has maintained that she does. God used that baby girl to fill a huge hole in my heart. From the time she was tiny and could recognize faces, she was always delighted to see her Grammy.

Grammy playing with Susanna and Alyssa

My house went on the market in April and sold by August. It took a while for me to adjust to living with Mike and MaryKay, not because of them but because of me. I didn't know where I fit without Dan. I didn't know who I was without him. God reminded me frequently that he was more than enough for me. For a time, I unwittingly expected my kids to fill the hole in my heart, but they were busy with their own families, and it wasn't their job. Many times I'd get frustrated because I felt invisible. God once again reminded me that I am loved by Him and never alone.

Deciding to live each day to the fullest, I paced myself so that I could enjoy each day thoroughly. I travelled more to see people I'd lost touch with or hadn't seen in a long time. My fiftieth class reunion from nursing school was held on a cruise ship heading to the Caribbean. I had not seen many of my classmates since graduation and decided to go. A few of my classmates were also widowed, and it felt good to connect with them on that level.

A few months later I was subbing at a Bible study and leading a group of ladies that I didn't know. In an attempt to build a bond with these women I asked them to say their names, whether or not they attended this particular church, and one thing about themselves. I started. "My name is Gloria; I attend this church and my husband died fifteen months ago."

A lady across the table elbowed the woman next to her and said, "Her too."

"Her too, what?" I asked.

"Her husband died fifteen months ago too." Nancy introduced herself to me, and we decided to meet for coffee soon. We became fast friends, both having similar life stories and feeling a lot of the same things. On the second anniversary of Dan's death and very close to the anniversary of Nancy's husband Sam's, we decided to take a trip to Lancaster, Pennsylvania to make new memories of things we had done with our husbands. We stayed in the same hotel Nancy and Sam had last stayed and went to Sight and Sound Theater to see the last show Dan and I had seen together.

Although it was bittersweet for both of us, God was healing our hearts little by little. We even took pictures of our respective husbands with us to share with one another, and neither of us had ever met the other spouse. Tears flowed freely, but the laughter took over as we shared funny stories about our lives as wives. Later we met each other's families and connected like we'd been long-time family friends. Nancy fell in love with one of my grandsons and prays for him faithfully every day. I was even invited on a family cruise with all of them.

"I need you to go with me Gloria. I cannot stand the idea of being in a cabin by myself without Sam," Nancy said as she sensed my indecisiveness. I wasn't sure it was a wise idea because I hadn't been responding well to the chemo I was on and really wasn't feeling that well. My doctor had sent me for a consult at Roswell in Buffalo to determine what my chemo regimen should be. She wanted to start it soon, and when I told her I had a cruise scheduled, she encouraged me to go.

Nancy seemed so adamant that she wanted me to go with her that I said I would. I spent a few days with Dan's sister Betty and her husband Bob, visited my friends Doris and Ron for a day, and then boarded the ship. All went well for the first four days, and then I was so sick I didn't even get out of bed. The next day I dragged myself to a pharmacia in Cozumel to get sinus medication and Tylenol for my fever, cough, and stuffy head. I skipped all meals until the last night and only went to thank everyone for inviting me to join them on the cruise. The next morning as we disembarked, I could hardly navigate. Bob saw me from the car trudging along dragging my suitcase and ran to help,

"You look awful," he exclaimed. "I think we need to take you directly to a hospital," he added obviously very concerned.

"I'll be all right Bob. I just need to lie down for a while."

We stopped for lunch on the way back to their home and chatted about the cruise. I did go right to bed as soon as we arrived at their house. They both kept checking on me periodically, obviously worried. Three days later as I was confirming my plane reservation to return home, Bob asked me if I was going to ask for a wheelchair in Orlando and Atlanta.

"They're big airports, Gloria, and you're in no condition to be walking from one concourse to another." Reluctantly I agreed as I hated appearing "needy." Old issues do crop up at the most inopportune times. I was so glad I listened to and took Bob's advice. Tipping my escorts was a privilege as I had no idea how much I'd appreciate my "ride." I had not requested a wheelchair when I arrived back in Syracuse, forgetting just how far the walk was from the gate to baggage claims. By the time I got there I was very short of breath. Mike had come to pick me up, took one look at me, and commanded me to sit down. He retrieved my luggage, and we walked out to the car.

The next morning he took me to the doctor, and I was immediately admitted to the hospital as my blood count was very low. I received four units of blood and began the new chemo. I also had a nasty bronchitis for which I received antibiotics. I had been reluctant to start the new chemo as it had the potential to wipe out what was left of my immune system. A few of my children encouraged me to have a quality of life rather than subjecting myself to the chemo. After much prayer I really felt like the Lord was saying I should at least try it, so I did. I also prayed that He would allow me to live long enough to experience my first great-grandchild. Kelly's daughter Katie was married but not expecting yet. After four months of treatments, I felt better than I had in ten years and thoroughly enjoyed every day, not knowing how long my remission would be. By pacing myself and helping others at times, I began to appreciate feeling better more joyfully than I ever had.

One year later, I was staying with my friend Nancy at her home when Katie face-timed me with her positive pregnancy test. I was elated and cried on and off for two days. God had answered my prayer once again.

Kelly and Ken's children: Zak, Katie, and Emily at Niagara Falls with us

# CHAPTER 24

I t has now been almost three years in remission, and I still feel great comparatively. I'm beginning to believe that after more than thirty-five years of dealing with illness the Lord may very well have healed me. My doctor responded to that remark with, "You are definitely doing well now." She has no idea how long my remission will last, but I'm believing forever.

Like a seasoned citizen, I reside in my declining years grateful for the life God has given me. Psalm 139 is my very favorite. It speaks of God knowing me so well that He knows when I sit down and when I rise; He knit me together in my mother's womb; that I have been fearfully and wonderfully made; that all the days for me were written in His book before one of them came to be. If I were to write a thesis statement for that Psalm it would be: there are no mistakes in God's economy. None!

All that I experienced in life has made me into the woman that I am. Some of my trials were hard; of that there is no doubt, but some have been joyful as well. My childhood, marriage, children, employment, and widowhood have been used by God to prepare me for His Eternal Kingdom. His gracious hand has been upon me throughout my life even before I knew Jesus and his atoning sacrifice for my sins. I have no idea what he has protected me from or guided me through the years, but am certain that left to my own devices, I would have strayed far. I know deep in my heart that should I die tomorrow, I will immediately be in His presence. I am so free of all the walls I erected to protect myself. I no longer need them as I am still becoming all He's designed me to be.

My question for you, my reader, is do you have that assurance? You can by realizing that God loves you so much that He sent his beloved Son to pay the penalty for your sins, past, present, and future. For years I had heard those truths in my head but not in my heart until a dear friend had the courage to hand me a book with an invitation at the end. I am so glad that I heard the Lord calling my name and responded. You can do the same by listening for His voice calling you, repenting of your sins, and asking Jesus to come into your heart and be your Lord and Savior. There is no guarantee of a smooth sailing life afterwards, but there is a power beyond yourself to help you cope with living in a fallen world. If you'd like the assurance of knowing Jesus, I invite you to pray the following prayer with your whole heart, mind, soul, and strength.

Dear Jesus,

I know that I'm a sinner and deserving of death. I turn from my sinful ways and ask You to forgive me. Thank you for dying on the cross in my place. Please come into my heart and be my Lord and Savior. Help me to follow You all the days of my life.

In Jesus Name and for His Glory, Amen.

You are now a child of the King and will spend eternity in Heaven with Him. Things will not always go smoothly. Hang in there; find a Bible-believing church and read a little bit of your Bible every day. The Holy Spirit who now resides inside of you will be your guide and teacher. Write on the inside cover of your Bible the date you prayed the above prayer and celebrate that day every year of your life.

Know you are loved with an everlasting love

# ACKNOWLEDGEMENTS

M any people have been instrumental in encouraging me to write and have prayed me through the process. I want to especially thank my good friend Sally Stuart who saw my potential almost thirty years ago when I first met her at a writer's conference in Chicago. She has nagged, cajoled, and prodded my stubborn self for many years. She also edited my entire manuscript with encouragement and very helpful suggestions. Two other people who also edited and made many comments that tightened the content of my story are Ron Short and Lois Eddy. Their comments and laborious critique were wonderfully received. Thanks also to Laurie Hartman and Joyce Dunn for praying continuously for me as I struggled at times to move forward. Laurie also scanned all the photos for me as I am semi-computer-illiterate. Thanks also to my small group, my pastors, many dear friends, and family who have prayed continuously for me. The people at Xulon Press have been so very helpful and encouraging. Thank you each and every one.

Last, and most importantly, I thank my Lord and Savior, Jesus Christ for saving my wretched soul and making me into the woman He created me to be. To Him be the glory forever and ever. Amen

Printed in the USA
CPSIA information can be obtained
at www.ICGtesting.com
LVHW012007181123
764329LV00009B/1309

9 781498 431552